Chronicles of England, Scotland and Ireland (2 of 6) England (1 of 12) William the Conqueror • Holinshed, Raphael, -1580?

Publisher's Note

Purchase of this book entitles you to a free trial membership in the publisher's book club at www.rarebooksclub.com. (Time limited offer.) Simply enter the barcode number from the back cover onto the membership form on our home page. The book club entitles you to select from millions of books at no additional charge. You can also download a digital copy of this and related books to read on the go. Simply enter the title or subject onto the search form to find them.

Note: This is an historic book. Pages numbers, where present in the text, refer to the first edition of the book and may also be in indexes.

If you have any questions, could you please be so kind as to consult our Frequently Asked Questions page at www.rarebooksclub.com/faqs.cfm? You are also welcome to contact us there.
Publisher: General Books LLC™, Memphis, TN, USA, 2012. ISBN: 9781153595797.
Proofreading: pgdp.net

※ ※ ※ ※ ※ ※ ※ ※

HOLINSHED'S

CHRONICLES

OF
  ENGLAND, SCOTLAND,
  AND
  IRELAND.
IN SIX VOLUMES.
VOL. II.
  ENGLAND.
LONDON:
  PRINTED FOR J. JOHNSON; F. C. AND J. RIVINGTON; T. PAYNE; WILKIE AND ROBINSON; LONGMAN, HURST, REES, AND ORME; CADELL AND DAVIES; AND J. MAWMAN.
1807.
AMS PRESS INC.
NEW YORK
1965
  AMS PRESS INC.
NEW YORK, N.Y. 10003
1965
  MANUFACTURED in the U.S.A.
  [*Original Title.*]
  THE
  THIRD VOLUME
  OF
  CHRONICLES,
  BEGINNING AT
  DUKE WILLIAM THE NORMAN, COMMONLIE CALLED THE CONQUEROR;
  AND
  DESCENDING BY DEGREES OF YEERES
  TO ALL THE
  KINGS AND QUEENES OF ENGLAND
  IN THEIR
  ORDERLIE SUCCESSIONS:
  FIRST COMPILED BY
  RAPHAELL HOLINSHED,
  AND BY HIM EXTENDED TO THE
  YEARE 1577.
  NOW NEWLIE RECOGNISED, AUGMENTED, AND CONTINUED
  (WITH OCCURRENCES AND ACCIDENTS OF FRESH MEMORIE)
  TO THE YEARE 1586.
  WHEREIN ALSO ARE CONTEINED MANIE MATTERS OF SINGULAR DISCOURSE
  AND RARE OBSERUATION,
  FRUITFULL TO SUCH AS BE STUDIOUS IN ANTIQUITIES,
  OR
  TAKE PLEASURE IN THE GROUNDS OF ANCIENT HISTORIES.
  With a third table (peculiarlie seruing this third volume) both of names and matters memorable.
HISTORIÆ PLACEANT NOSTRATES AC PEREGRINÆ
  TO THE
  RIGHT HONORABLE AND HIS SINGULAR GOOD LORD,
  SIR WILLIAM CECILL,
  BARON OF BURGHLEYGH, KNIGHT OF THE MOST NOBLE ORDER OF THE GARTER, LORD HIGH TREASURER OF ENGLAND, MAISTER OF THE COURTS OF WARDS AND LIUERIES, AND ONE OF THE QUEENES MAIESTIES PRIUIE COUNCELL.

Considering with my selfe, right Honorable and my singular good Lord, how redie (no doubt) manie will be to accuse me of vaine presumption, for enterprising to deale in this so weightie a worke, and so far aboue my reach to accomplish: I haue thought good to aduertise your Honour, by what occasion I was first induced to vndertake the same, although the cause that moued me thereto hath (in part) yer this beene signified vnto your good Lordship.

Whereas therefore, that worthie Citizen Reginald Wolfe late Printer to the Queenes Maiestie, a man well knowne and beholden to your Honour, meant in his life time to publish an vniuersall Cosmographie of the whole world, and therewith also certaine particular histories of euery knowne nation, amongst other whom he purposed to vse for performance of his intent in that behalfe, he procured me to take in hand the collection of those histories, and hauing proceeded so far in the same, as little wanted to the accomplishment of that long promised worke, it pleased God to call him to his mercie, after fiue and twentie yeares trauell spent therein; so that by his vntimelie deceasse, no hope remained to see that performed, which we had so long trauelled about. Neuerthelesse those whom he put in trust to dispose his things after his departure hence, wishing to the benefit of others, that some fruit might follow of that whereabout he had imployed so long time, willed me to continue mine indeuour for their furtherance in the same. Which although I was redie to doo, so far as mine abilitie would reach, and the rather to answere that trust which the deceassed reposed in me, to see it brought to some perfection: yet when the volume grew so great as they that were to defraie the charges for the impression, were not willing to go through the whole, they resolued first to publish the histories of England, Scotland, and Ireland, with their descriptions; which descriptions, bicause they were not in such readinesse, as those of forren countries, they were inforced to vse the helpe of other better able to doo it than my selfe.

Moreouer, the Charts, wherein Maister Wolfe spent a great part of his time, were not found so complet as we wished: and againe, vnderstanding of the great charges and notable enterprise of that worthie Gentleman maister Thomas Sackford, in procuring the Charts of the seuerall prouinces of this realme to be set foorth, we are in hope that in time he will delineate this whole land so perfectlie, as shall be comparable or beyond anie delineation heretofore made of anie other region; and therefore leaue that to his well deserued praise. If any well willer will imitate him in so praiseworthie a worke for the two other regions, we will be glad to further his endeuour with all the helpes we may.

The histories I haue gathered according to my skill, and conferred the greatest part with Maister Wolfe in his life time, to his liking, who procured me so manie helpes to the furtherance thereof, that I was loth to omit anie thing that might increase the readers knowledge, which causeth the booke to grow so great. But receiuing them by parts, and at seuerall times (as I might get them) it may be, that hauing had more regard to the matter than the apt penning, I haue not so orderlie disposed them, as otherwise I ought; choosing rather to want order, than to defraud the reader of that which for his further vnderstanding might seeme to satisfie his expectation.

I therefore most humblie beseech your Honour to accept these Chronicles of England vnder your protection, and according to your wisedome and accustomed benignitie to beare with my faults; the rather, bicause you were euer so especiall good Lord to Maister Wolfe, to whom I was singularlie beholden; and in whose name I humblie present this rude worke vnto you; beseeching God, that as he hath made you an instrument to aduance his truth, so it may please him to increase his good gifts in you, to his glorie, the furtherance of the Queenes Maiesties seruice, and the comfort of all hir faithfull and louing subiects.

Your Honours most humble to be commanded,

Raphael Holinshed

THE
PREFACE TO THE READER.

It is dangerous (gentle reader) to range in so large a field as I haue here vndertaken, while so manie sundrie men in diuers things may be able to controll me, and manie excellent wits of our countrie (as well or better occupied I hope) are able herein to surpasse me; but seeing the best able doo seeme to neglect it, let me (though least able) craue pardon to put them in mind not to forget their natiue countries praise (which is their dutie) the incouragement of their woorthie countriemen, by elders aduancements; and the daunting of the vicious, by foure penall examples, to which end (as I take it) chronicles and histories ought cheefelie to be written. My labour may shew mine vttermost good will, of the more learned I require their further enlargement, and of faultfinders dispensation till they be more fullie informed. It is too common that the least able are readiest to find fault in matters of least weight, and therefore I esteeme the lesse of their carping, but humblie beseech the skilfull to supplie my want, and to haue care of their dutie; and either to amend that wherein I haue failed, or be content with this mine endeuour. For it may please them to consider, that no one can be eie-witnesse to all that is written within our time; much lesse to those things which happened in former times, and therefore must be content with reports of others. Therein I haue beene so carefull, that I haue spared no paines or helpe of freends to search out either written or printed ancient authors, or to inquire of moderne eie-witnesses for the true setting downe of that which I haue here deliuered: but I find such want in writers for the necessarie knowledge of things doone in times past, and lacke of meanes to obteine sufficient instructions by reporters of the time present; and herewith the worthie exploits of our countriemen so manie, that it greeueth me I could not leaue the same to posteritie (as I wished) to their well deserued praise. But I haue here imparted what I could learne, and craue that it may be taken in good part. My speech is plaine, without any rhetoricall shew of eloquence, hauing rather a regard to simple truth, than to decking words. I wish I had beene furnished with so perfect instructions, and so many good gifts, that I might haue pleased all kinds of men, but that same being so rare a thing in any one of the best, I beseech thee (gentle reader) not to looke for it in me the meanest.

But now for thy further instruction, to vnderstand the course of these my labours. First concerning the historie of England, as I haue collected the same out of manie and sundrie authors, in whome what contrarietie, negligence, and rashnesse sometime is found in their reports; I leaue to the discretion of those that haue perused their works: for my part, I haue in things doubtfull rather chosen to shew the diuersitie of their writings, than by ouer-ruling them, and vsing a peremptorie censure, to frame them to agree to my liking: leauing it neuerthelesse to each mans iudgement, to controll them as he seeth cause. If some-where I shew my fansie what I thinke, and that the same dislike them; I craue pardon, speciallie if by probable reasons or plainer matter to be produced, they can shew mine errour; vpon knowledge whereof I shall be readie to reforme it accordinglie. Where I doo begin the historic from the first inhabitation of this Ile, I looke not to content ech mans opinion concerning the originall of them that first peopled it, and no maruell: for in matters so vncerteine, if I cannot sufficientlie content my selfe (as in deed I cannot) I know not how I should satisfie others. That which seemeth to me most likelie, I haue noted, beseeching the learned (as I trust they will) in such points of doubtfull antiquities to beare with my skill: sith for ought I know, the matter is not yet decided among the learned, but still they are in controuersie about it, and as yet Sub iudice lis est. Well, howsoeuer it came first to be inhabited, likelie it is, that at the first the whole Ile was vnder one prince and gouernour, though afterwards (and long peraduenture before the Romans set any foot within it) the monarchie thereof was broken, euen when the multitude of the inhabitants grew to be great, and ambition entred amongst them: which hath brought so manie good policies and states to ruine and decaie.

The Romans hauing once got possession of the continent that faceth this Ile, could not rest (as it appeareth) till they had brought the same also vnder their subiection: and the sooner doubtlesse, by reason of the factions amongst the princes of the land, which the Romans (through their accustomed skill) could turne verie well to their most aduantage. They possessed it almost fiue hundreth yeares, and longer might haue doone, if either their insufferable tyrannie had not taken awaie from them the loue of the people as well here as else-where; either that their ciuill discord about the chopping and changing of their emperours had not so weakened the forces of their empire, that they were not able to defend the same against the irruption of barbarous nations. But as we may coniecture by that which is found in histories, about that time, in which the Romane empire began to decline, this land stood in verie weake state: being spoiled of the most part of all hir able men, which were led

[1] 25

awaie into forren regions, to supplie the Romane armies; and likewise (perhaps) of all necessarie armour, weapon, and treasure: which being perceiued of the Saxons, after they were receiued into the Ile, to aid the Britons against the Scots and Picts then inuading the same, ministred to them occasion to attempt the second conquest, which at length they brought to passe, to the ouerthrow not onelie of the British dominion, but also to the subuersion of the Christian religion here in this land: which chanced (às appeareth by Gildas) for the wicked sins and vnthankefulnesse of the inhabitants towards God, the cheefe occasions and causes of the transmutations of kingdoms, Nam propter peccata, regna transmatantur à gente in gentem.

The Saxons obteining possession of the land, gouerned the same, being diuided into sundrie kingdoms, and hauing once subdued the Britons, or at the least-wise remooued them out of the most part of the Ile into od corners and mountaines; fell at diuision among themselues, and oftentimes with warre pursued ech other, so as no perfect order of gouernement could be framed, nor the kings grow to any great puissance, either to mooue warres abroad, or sufficientlie to defend themselues against forren forces at home: as manifestlie was perceiued; when the Danes and other the Northeasterne people, being then of great puissance by sea, began misserablie to afflict this land: at the first inuading as it were but onelie the coasts and countries lieng neere to the sea, but afterwards with manie armies they entred into the midle parts of the land. And although the English people at length came vnder one king, and by that meanes were the better able to resist the enimies; yet at length those Danes subdued the whole, and had possession thereof for a time although not long, but that the crowne returned againe to those of the Saxon line: till shortlie after, by the insolent dealings of the gouernours, a diuision was made betwixt the king and his people, through iust punishment decreed by

the prouidence of the Almightie, determining for their sinnes and contempt of his lawes, to deliuer them into the hands of a stranger; and thereupon when spite and enuie had brought the title in doubt, to whom the right in succession apperteined, the Conquerour entred, and they remained a prey to him and his: who plucked all the heads and cheefe in authoritie so cleerelie vp by the roots, as few or none of them in the end was left to stand vp against him. And herewith altering the whole state, he planted such lawes and ordinances as stood most for his auaile and securitie, which being after qualified with more milde and gentle lawes, tooke such effect, that the state hath euer sithens continued whole and vnbroken by wise and politike gouernement, although disquieted sometime by ciuill dissention, to the ruine commonlie of the first moouers, as by the sequele of the historie you may see.

For the historie of Scotland, I haue for the more part followed Hector Boece, Iohannes Maior, and Iouan Ferreri Piemontese, so far as they haue continued it, interlaced somtimes with other authours, as Houeden, Fourdon, and such like; although not often, bicause I meant rather to deliuer what I found in their owne histories extant, than to correct them by others, leauing that enterprise to their owne countrimen: so that whatsoeuer ye read in the same, consider that a Scotishman writ it, and an Englishman hath but onelie translated it into our language, referring the reader to the English historie, in all matters betwixt vs and them, to be confronted therewith as he seeth cause. For the continuation thereof I vsed the like order, in such copies and notes as Maister Wolfe in his life time procured me; sauing that in these last yeares I haue inserted some such notes as concerned matters of warre betwixt vs and the Scots, bicause I got them not till that part of the English historie was past the presse.

For Ireland, I haue shewed in mine epistle dedicatorie in what sort, and by what helps I haue proceeded therein; onelie this I forgot to signifie, that I had not Giraldus Cambrensis, and Flatsburie, vntill that part of the booke was vnder the presse, and so being constreined to make post hast, I could not exemplifie what I would out of them all, neither yet dispose it so orderlie as had beene conuenient, nor pen it with so apt words as might satisfie either my-selfe, or those to whose view it is now like to come. And by reason of the like haste made in the impression, where I was determined to haue transposed the most part of that which in the English historie I had noted, concerning the conquest of Ireland by Hen. the second, out of Houeden & others, I had not time thereto; and so haue left it there remaining where I first noted it, before I determined to make any particular collection of the Irish histories, bicause the same commeth there well inough in place, as to those that shall vouchsafe to turne the booke it may appeare.

For the computation of the yeares of the world, I had by Maister Wolfes aduise followed Functius; but after his deceasse, M. W. H. made me partaker of a Chronologie, which he had gathered and compiled with most exquisit diligence, following Gerardus Mercator, and other late Chronologers, and his owne obseruations, according to the which I haue reformed the same. As for the yeares of our Lord, and the kings, I haue set them downe according to such authors as seeme to be of best credit in that behalfe, as I doubt not but the learned and skilfull in histories it shall appeare. Moreouer, this the reader hath to consider, that I doo begin the yeare at the natiuitie of our Lord, which is the surest order (in my fansie) that can be followed.

For the names of persons, townes, and places, as I haue beene diligent to reforme the errours of other (which are to be ascribed more to the vnperfect copies than to the authors) so may it be that I haue some-where committed the like faults, either by negligence or want of skill to restore them to their full integritie as I wished. But what I haue performed, aswell in that behalfe as others, the skilfull reader shall easily perceiue, and withall consider (I trust) what trauell I haue bestowed to his behoofe in this huge volume; crauing onelie, that in recompense thereof he will iudge the best, and to make a freendlie construction of my meaning, where ought may seeme to haue escaped my pen or the printers presse, otherwise than we could haue wished for his better satisfaction. Manie things being taken out as they lie in authors, may be thought to giue offense in time present, which referred to the time past when the author writ, are not onelie tollerable, but also allowable. Therefore (good reader) I beseech thee to weigh the causes and circumstances of such faults and imperfections, and consider that the like may creepe into a far lesse volume than this, and shew me so much fauour as hath beene shewed to others in like causes. And sithens I haue doone my good will, accept the same, as I with a free and thankefull mind doo offer it thee; so shall I thinke my labour well bestowed. For the other histories, which are alreadie collected, if it please God to giue abilitie, shall in time come to light, with some such breefe descriptions of the forren regions whereof they treat, as may the better suffice to the readers contentation, and vnderstanding of the matters conteined in the same histories, reduced into abridgements out of their great volumes. And thus I ceasse further to trouble thy patience, wishing to thee (gentle reader) so much profit, as by reading may be had, and as great comfort as Gods holie spirit may endue thee with.

FINIS.

[1]

THE POLITIKE CONQUEST OF WILLIAM THE FIRST.

Anno 1. This William Duke of Normandie, base son of Robert the sixt Duke of Normandie, and nephew vnto Edward king of England, surnamed the Confessor, hauing vanquished the English power, and slaine Harold in the field (as you may read at large towards the end of the historie of England) began his reigne ouer England the xv. daie of October being Sundaie, in the yeare after the creation of the world 5033, (as 1066. W. Harison gathereth) and after the birth of our Sauiour 1066, which was in the tenth yeare of the emperour Henrie the fourth, in the sixt of pope Alexander the second, in the sixt of Philip king of France, and about the tenth of Malcolme the third, surnamed Camoir, king of Scotland.

Sim. Dun. Immediatlie after he had thus got the victorie in a pight field (as before ye haue heard) he first returned to Hastings, and after set forward towards London, wasted the countries of Sussex, Kent, Hamshire, Southerie, Middlesex, and Herefordshire, burning the townes, and sleaing the people, till he came to Beorcham. In the meane time, immediatlie after the discomfiture in Sussex, the two earles of Northumberland and Edwin and Marchar.

Quéene Aldgitha sent to Chester.

Wil. Mal. Simon Dun. Mercia, Edwin and Marchar, who had withdrawne themselues from the battell togither with their people, came to London, and with all speed sent their sister quéene Aldgitha vnto the citie of Chester, and herewith sought to persuade the Londoners to aduance one of them to the kingdome: as Wil. Mal. writeth. But Simon of Durham saith, that Aldred archbishop of Yorke, and the said earles with others would haue made Edgar Etheling king. Howbeit, whilest manie of the Nobilitie and others prepared to make themselues redie to giue a new battell to the Normans (how or whatsoeuer was the cause) the said earles drew homewards with their powers, to the great discomfort *Wil. Malm.* The bishops blamed. of their freends. Wil. Malm. séemeth to put blame in the bishops, for that the lords went not forward with their purpose in aduancing Edgar Etheling to the crowne. For the bishops (saith he) refused to ioine with the lords in that behalfe, and so through enuie and spite which one part bare to another, when they could not agrée vpon an The archbishop of Yorke & other submit themselues to king William. Englishman, they receiued a stranger, insomuch that vpon king William his comming vnto Beorcham, Aldred archbishop of Yorke, Wolstane bishop of Worcester, and Walter bishop of Hereford, Edgar Etheling, and the foresaid earles Edwin and Marchar came and submitted themselues vnto him, whom he gentlie receiued, and incontinentlie made an agréement with them, taking their oth and hostages (as some write) and yet neuerthelesse he permitted his people to spoile and burne the countrie.

But now, when the feast of Christs natiuitie (commonlie called Christmas) was at hand, he approched to the citie of London, and comming thither, caused his vauntgard first to enter into the stréets, where finding some resistance, he easilie subdued the citizens that thus tooke vpon them to withstand him, though not without some bloudshed *Gemeticensis.* (as Gemeticen. writeth) but as by others it should appéere, he was receiued into the [2] citie without anie resistance at all; and so being in possession thereof, he spake manie fréendlie words to the citizens, and promised that he would vse them in most liberall William Conquerour crowned 1067, according to their account which begin the yeare on the daie of Christ his natiuitie. & courteous maner. Not long after, when things were brought in order (as was thought requisite) he was crowned king vpon Christmas daie following, by Aldred archbishop of Yorke. For he would not receiue the crowne at the hands of Stigand archbishop of Canturburie, bicause he was hated, and furthermore iudged to be a verie lewd person and a naughtie liuer.

At his coronation he caused the bishops and barons of the realme to take their oth, that they should be his true and loiall subiects (according to the maner in that case accustomed.) And being required thereto by the archbishop of Yorke, he tooke his personall oth before the altar of S. Peter at Westmister, to defend the holie church, and rulers of the same, to gouerne the people in iustice as became a king to doo, to ordeine righteous lawes & kéepe the same, so that all maner of bribing, rapine, and wrongful iudgements should for euer after be abolished.

Polydor. 1067. After this, he tooke order how to keepe the realme in good and quiet gouernment, fortifieng the necessarie places, and furnishing them with garisons. He also appointed officers and councellers, such as he thought to be wise and discréet men, and appointed ships to be in the hauens by the coast for the defense of the land, as he thought moste *Iohn Stow.* expedient. After his coronation, or rather before (as by some authours it should *Thos. Spot.* seeme) euen presentlie vpon obteining of the citie of London, he tooke his iourney towards the castell of Douer, to subdue that and the rest of Kent also: which when the archbishop Stigand and Egelsin the abbat of S. Augustines (being as it were the chiefest lords and gouernours of all Kent) did perceiue, and considered that the whole realme was in an euill state; & that whereas in this realme of England, before the Seruitude & bondage of the Nobilitie and Commonaltie to the Normans. comming in of the forsaid duke William, there were no bondmen: now all, as well the Nobilitie as the Commonaltie were without respect made subiect to the intollerable bondage of the Normans, taking an occasion by the perill and danger that their neighbours were in, to prouide for the safegard of themselues and their countrie. They caused all the people of the countie of Kent to assemble at Canturburie, and declared to them the perils and dangers imminent, the miserie that their neighbours were come into, the pride and insolencie of the Normans, and the hardnesse and griefe of bondage and seruile estate. Whereupon all the people rather choosing to end their vnfortunate life, than to submit themselues to an vnaccustomed yoke of seruitude and bondage, with a common consent determined to méet duke William, and to fight with him for the lawes of their countrie. Also, the foresaid Stigand the archbishop, and the abbat Egelsin, choosing rather to die in battell, than to see their nation in so euill an estate, being encouraged by the examples of the holie Machabées, became capteins of the armie. And at a daie appointed, all the people met at Swanescombe, and being hidden in the woods, laie priuilie in wait for the comming of the foresaid duke William.

Now, bicause it cannot hurt to take great héed, and to be verie warie in such cases, they agréed before hand, that when the duke was come, and the passages on euerie side stopped, to the end he should no waie be able to escape, euerie one of them, as well horssemen as footmen should beare boughes in their hands. The next daie after, when the duke was come into the fields and territories néere vnto Swanescombe, and saw all the countrie set and placed about him, as it had beene a stirring and moouing wood, and that with a meane pace they approched and drew neare vnto him, with great discomfort of mind he woondered at that sight. And assoone as the capteins of the Kentishmen sawe that duke William was inclosed in the middest of their armie, they caused their trumpets to be sounded, their banners to be displaied, and threw downe their boughes, & with their bowes bent, their swords drawne, and their speares and other kind of weapons stretched foorth, they shewed themselues readie to fight. Duke William and they that were with him stood (as no maruell it was) sore astonied, and amazed: [3] so that he which thought he had alreadie all England fast in his fist, did now despaire of his owne life. Therefore on the behalfe of the Kentishmen, were sent vnto duke William the archbishop Stigand, and Egelsin abbat of S. Augustines, who told him their message in this sort.

"My lord duke, behold the people of Kent come forth to méet you, and to receiue you as their liege lord, requiring at your hands the things which perteine to peace, and that vnder this condition; that all the people of Kent enioy for euer their ancient liberties, and may for euermore vse the lawes and customes of the countrie: otherwise they are readie presentlie to bid battell to you, and them that be with you, and are minded rather to die here altogither, than to depart from the lawes and customes of their countrie, and to submit themselues to bondage, whereof as yet they neuer had experience."

The duke séeing himselfe to be driuen to such an exigent & narrow pinch, consulted a while with them that came with him, prudentlie considering, that if he should take anie repulse or displeasure at the hands of this people, which be the key of England, all that he had done before should be disanulled and made of none effect, and all his hope and safetie should stand in danger and ieopardie: not so willinglie as wiselie he granted the people of Kent their request. Now when the couenant was established, and pledges giuen on both sides: the Kentishmen being ioyfull, conducted the Normans (who also were glad) vnto Rochester, and yéelded vp to the duke the earledome of Kent, and the noble castell of Douer. Thus the ancient liberties of England, and the lawes and customes of the countrie, which before the comming of duke William out of Normandie, were equallie kept throughout all England, doo (through this industrie and earnest trauell of the archbishop Stigand and Egelsin abbat of S. Augustines) remaine inuiolablie obserued vntill this daie within that countie of Kent. ¶ Thus far Thomas Spot, and after him William Thorne writeth the same. Of the which the former (that is Spot) liued in the daies of king Edward the first, and William Thorne in the daies of king Richard the second.

The ancient liberties and lawes of England remaine in Kent onlie. *Wil. Thorne.*

But now, before we procéed anie further in recitall of the Conquerours dooings, we haue here in a table noted all the noble capteins and gentlemen of name, aswell Normans as other strangers, which assisted duke William in the conquest of this land: and first, as we find them written in the chronicles of Normandie by one William Tailleur.

THE CATALOG OF SUCH NOBLEMEN, LORDS, AND GENTLEMEN OF NAME, AS CAME INTO THIS LAND WITH WILLIAM THE CONQUEROUR.

Odo bishop of Bayeulx.
Robert erle of Mortaing.
Roger erle of Beaumont surnamed *A la Barbe.*
Guillaume Mallet seigneur de Montfort.
Henrie seig. de Ferrers.
Guillaume d'Aubelle-mare seign. de Fougieres.
Guillaume de Roumare seig. de Lithare.
Le seig. de Touque.
Le seig. de la Mare.
Neel le Viconte.
Guillaume de Vepont.
Le seig. de Magneuille.
Le seig. de Grosmenil.
Le seig. de S. Martin.
Le seig. de Puis.
Guillaume Crespin.
Guillaume de Movenne.
Guillaume Desmoulins.
Guillaume Desgarennes.
Hue de Gourney, *aliàs* Genevay.
Le seig. de Bray.
Le seig. de Gouy.
Le seig. de Laigle.
Le seig. de Touarts.
Le seig. de Aurenchin.
Le seig. de Vitrey.
Le seig. de Trassy, *aliàs* Tracy.
Le seig. de Picquigny.
Le seig. d'Espinay.
Osmond seig. du Pont.
Le seig. de Estouteuile.
Le seig. de Torchy.
Le seig. de Barnabost.
Le seig. de Breual.
Le seig. de Seeulme.
Le seig. de Houme.
Le seig. de Souchoy.
Le seig. de Cally.
Le seig. de la Riuere.
Euldes de Beanieu.
Le seig. de Roumilly.
Le seig. de Glotz.
Le seig. du Sap.
Le seig. de Vanuille.
Le seig. Branchou.
Le seig. Balleul.
Le seig. de Beausault.
Le seig. de Telleres.
Le seig. de Senlys.
Le seig. de Bacqueuille.
Le seig. de Preaulx.
Le seig. de Iouy.
Le seig. de Longueuille.
Le seig. de Aquigny.
Le seig. de Passy.
Le seig. de Tournay.
Le seig. de Colombieres.
Le seig. de Bolleber.
Le seig. de Garensieres.
Le seig. de Longueile.
Le seig. de Houdetot.
Le seig. de Malletot.
Le seig. de la Haie Malerbe.
Le seig. de Porch Pinche.
Le seig. de Iuetot.
The erle of Tanqueruile.
The erle d'Eu.
The erle d'Arques.
The erle of Aniou.
The erle of Neuers.
Le seig. de Rouuile.
Le prince de Alemaigne.
Le seig. de Pauilly.
Le seig. de S. Cler.
Le seig. d'Espinay.
Le seig. de Bremetot.
Alain Fergant erle of Britaigne.
Le seig. de la Ferte.
Robert fils Heruays duc de Orleans.
Le seig. de la Lande.
Le seig. de Mortimer.
Le seig. de Clare.
Le seig. de Magny.
Le seig. de Fontnay.
Roger de Montgomery.
Amaury de Touars.
Le seig. de Hacqueuile.
Le seig. de Neanshou.
Le seig. de Perou.
Robert de Beaufou.
Le seig. Meauuon.
Le seig. de Soteuile.
Eustace de Hambleuile.
Geoffray Bournom.
Le seig. de Blainuile.
Le seig. de Maueuile.
Geoffrey de Moienne.
Auffray and Mauger de Carteny.
Le seig. de Freanuile.
Le seig. de Moubray.
Le seig. de Iafitay.
Guillaume Patais seig. de la Lande.
Eulde de Mortimer.
Hue erle of Gournay.
Egremont de Laigle.
Richard d'Aurinchin.
Le seig. de Bearts.
Le seig. de Soulligny.
Bouteclier d'Aubigny.
Le seig. de Marcey.
Le seig. de Lachy.
Le seig. de Valdere.
Eulde de Montfort.
Henoyn de Cahieu.

Le seig. de Vimers.
Guillaume de Mouion.
Raoul Tesson de Tignolles.
Anguerand erle of Hercourt.
Roger Marmion.
Raoul de Gaiel.
Auenel de Viers.
Pauuel du Montier Hubert.
Robert Bertraule Tort.
Le seig. de Seulle.
Le seig. Doriual.
Le seig. de la Hay.
Le seig. de S. Iohn.
Le seig. de Saussy.
Le seig. de Brye.
Richard Dollebec.
Le seig. du Monfiquet.
Le seig. de Bresey.
Le seig. de Semilly.
Le seig. de Tilly.
Le seig. de Preaux.
Le seig. de S. Denis.
Le seig. de Meuley.
Le seig. de Monceaux.
The archers of Bretuile.
The archers of Vaudreuile.
Le seig. de S. Sain.
Le seig. de Breansou.
Le seig. de Sassy.
Le seig. de Nassy.
Le vidam de Chartres.
Le seig. de Ieanuile.
Le vidam du Passais.
Pierre du Bailleul seig. de Fescampe.
Le seneschal de Torchy.
Le seig. de Grissey.
Le seig. de Bassey.
Le seig. de Tourneur.
Guillaume de Colombieres.
Le seig. de Bonnebault.
Le seig. de Ennebault.
Le seig. de Danuillers.
Le seig. de Beruile.
Le seig. de Creueceur.
Le seig. de Breate.
Le seig. de Coutray.
The erle of Eureux.
Le seig. de seint Valery.
Thomas erle d'Aumale.
The erle de Hiesmes.

[5] With other lords and men of account in great numbers, whose names the author of the chronicles of Normandie could not come by (as he himselfe confesseth.) In consideration whereof, and bicause diuers of these are set foorth onlie by their titles of estate, and not by their surnames; we haue thought it conuenient to make you partakers of the roll which sometime belonged to Battell abbeie, conteining also (as the title thereof importeth) the names of such Nobles and Gentlemen of Marque, as came at this time with the Conqueror, whereof diuerse maie be the same persons which in the catalog aboue written are conteined, bearing the names of the places whereof they were possessors and owners, as by the same catalog maie appeare.

THE ROLL OF BATTELL ABBEIE.
A
Avmarle
Aincourt
Audeley
Adgillam
Argentoune
Arundell
Auenant
Abell
Auuerne
Aunwers
Angers
Angenoun
Archere
Anuay
Asperu
Albeuile
Andeuile
Amouerduile
Arcy and Akeny
Albeny
Aybeuare
Amay
Aspermound
Amerenges
B
Bertram
Buttecourt
Brebus and Byseg
Bardolfe
Basset and Bigot
Bohun
Bailif
Bondeuile
Brabason
Baskeruile
Bures
Bounilaine
Bois
Botelere
Bourcher
Brabaion
Berners
Braibuf
Brande and Bronce
Burgh
Bushy
Banet
Blondell
Breton
Bluat and Baious
Browne
Beke
Bickard
Banastre
Baloun
Beauchampe
Bray and Bandy
Bracy
Boundes
Bascoun
Broilem
Broleuy
Burnell
Bellet
Baudewin
Beaumont
Burdon
Berteuilay
Barre
Busseuile
Blunt
Beaupere
Beuill
Barduedor
Brette
Barrett
Bonret
Bainard
Barniuale
Bonett
Barry
Bryan
Bodin
Beteruile
Bertin
Bereneuile
Bellewe
Beuery
Busshell
Boranuile
Browe
Beleuers
Buffard

Botelere
Bonueier
Boteuile
Bellire
Bastard
Bainard
Brasard
Beelhelme
Braine
Brent
Braunch
Belesuz
Blundell
Burdet
Bagot
Beauuise
Belemis
Beisin
Bernon
Boels
Belefroun
Brutz
Barchampe

C

Camois
Camuile
Chawent
Chauncy
Conderay
Coluile
Chamberlaine
Chamburnoun
Comin
Columber
Cribett
Creuquere
Corbine
Corbett
Chaundos
Chaworth
Cleremaus
Clarell
Chopis
Chaunduit
Chantelow
Chamberay
Cressy
Curtenay
Conestable
Cholmeley
Champney
Chawnos
Comiuile
Champaine
Careuile

Carbonelle
Charles
Chereberge
Chawnes
Chaumont
Caperoun
Cheine
Curson
Couille
Chaiters
Cheines
Cateray
Cherecourt
Cammile
Clerenay
Curly
Cuily
Clinels
Chaundos
Courteney
Clifford

D

Denauille
Dercy
Diue
Dispencere
Daubeny
Daniell
Denise and Druell
Deuans
Dauers
Dodingsels
Darell
Delaber
Delapole
Delalinde
Delahill
Delaware
Delauache
Dakeny
Dauntre
Desny
Dabernoune
Damry
Daueros
Dauonge
Duilby
Dalauere
Delahoid
Durange
Delee
Delaund
Delaward
Delaplanch
Damnot

Danway
Dehense
Deuile
Disard
Doiuille
Durant
Drury
Dabitot
Dunsteruile
Dunchampe
Dambelton

E

Estrange
Estuteuile
Engaine
Estriels
Esturney

F

Ferrerers
Foluille
Fitz Water
Fitz Marmaduke
Fleuez
Filberd
Fitz Roger
Fauecourt
Ferrers
Fitz Philip
Filiot
Furniueus
Furniuaus
Fitz Otes
Fitz William
Fitz Roand
Fitz Pain
Fitz Auger
Fitz Aleyn
Fitz Rauff
Fitz Browne
Fouke
Freuil
Front de Boef
Facunberge
Fort
Frisell
Fitz Simon
Fitz Fouk
Filioll
Fitz Thomas
Fitz Morice
Fitz Hugh
Fitz Henrie
Fitz Waren
Fitz Rainold
Flamuile

Formay	Herne	Lane
Fitz Eustach	Harecourt	Louetot
Fitz Laurence	Henoure	M
Formibaud	Houell	Mohant
Frisound	Hamelin	Mowne
Finere and Fitz Robert	Harewell	Maundeuile
Furniuale	Hardell	Marmilon
Fitz Geffrey	Haket	Moribray
Fitz Herbert	Hamound	Moruile
Fitz Peres	Harcord	Miriell
Fichet	I	Manlay
Fitz Rewes	Iarden	Malebraunch
Fitz Fitz	Iay	Malemame
Fitz John	Ieniels	Mortimere
Fleschampe	Ierconuise	Mortimaine
G	Ianuile	Muse
Gvrnay	Iasperuile	Marteine
Gressy	K	Mountbother
Graunson	Kaunt	Mountsoler
Gracy	Karre	Maleuile
Georges	Karrowe	Malet
Gower	Koine	Mounteney
Gaugy	Kimaronne	Monfichet
Goband	Kiriell	Maleherbe
Gray	Kancey	Mare
Gaunson	Kenelre	Musegros
Golofre	L	Musard
Gobion	Loueny	Moine
Grensy	Lacy	Montrauers
Graunt	Linneby	Merke
Greile	Latomer	Murres
Greuet	Loueday	Mortiuale
Gurry	Louell	Monchenesy
Gurley	Lemare	Mallory
Grammori	Leuetot	Marny
Gernoun	Lucy	Mountagu
Grendon	Luny	Mountford
Gurdon	Logeuile	Maule
Gines	Longespes	Monhermon
Griuil	Louerace	Musett
Greneuile	Longechampe	Meneuile
Glateuile	Lascales	Manteuenant and Manfe
Gurney	Lacy	Meapincoy
Giffard	Louan	Maine
Gouerges	Leded	Mainard
Gamages	Luse	Morell
H	Loterell	Mainell
Haunteney	Lornge	Maleluse
Haunsard	Longevule	Memorous
Hastings	Loy	Morreis
Hanlay	Lorancourt	Morleian Maine
Haurell	Loions	Maleuere
Husee	Limers	Mandut
Hercy	Longepay	Mountmarten
Herioun	Laumale	Mamelet

Miners
Mauclerke
Maunchenell
Mouet
Meintenore
Meletak
Manuile
Mangisere
Maumasin
Mountlouel
Mawreward
Monhaut
Meller
Mountgomerie
Manlay
Maulard
Mainard
Menere
Martinast
Mare
Mainwaring
Matelay
Malemis
Maleheire
Moren
Melun
Marceans
Maiell
Morton
N
Noers
Neuile
Newmarch
Norbet
Norice
Newborough
Neiremet
Neile
Normauile
Neofmarch
Nermitz
Nembrutz
O
Oteuell
Olibef
Olifant
Osenel
Oisell
Olifard
Orinall
Orioll
P
Pigot
Pery
Perepount

Pershale
Power
Painell
Perche and Pauey
Peurell
Perot
Picard
Pinkenie
Pomeray
Pounce
Pauely
Paifrere
Plukenet
Phuars
Punchardoun
Pinchard
Placy
Pugoy
Patefine
Place
Pampilioun
Percelay
Perere and Pekeny
Poterell
Peukeny
Peccell
Pinell
Putrill
Petiuoll
Preaus
Pantolf
Peito
Penecord
Preudirlegast
Perciuale
Q
Qvinci
Quintiny
R
Ros
Ridcll
Riuers
Riuell
Rous
Rushell
Raband
Ronde
Rie
Rokell
Risers
Randuile
Roselin
Rastoke
Rinuill
Rougere

Rait
Ripere
Rigny
Richemound
Rochford
Raimond
S
Souch
Sheuile
Seucheus
Senclere
Sent Quintin
Sent Omere
Sent Amond
Sent Legere
Someruile
Siward
Saunsovere
Sanford
Sanctes
Sauay
Saulay
Sules
Sorell
Somerey
Sent Iohn
Sent George
Sent Les
Sesse
Saluin
Say
Solers
Saulay
Sent Albin
Sent Martin
Sourdemale
Seguin
Sent Barbe
Sent Vile
Souremount
Sorcglisc
Sanduile
Sauncey
Sirewast
Sent Cheueroll
Sent More
Sent Scudemore
T
Toget
Tercy
Tuchet
Tracy
Trousbut
Trainell
Taket

Trussel and Trison
Talbot
Touny
Traies
Tollemach
Tolous
Tanny
Touke
Tibtote
Turbeuile
Turuile
Tomy and Taverner
Trencheuile
Trenchelion
Tankeruile
Tirell
Triuet
Tolet
Trauers
Tardeuile
Turburuile
Tineuile
Torell
Tortechappell
Trusbote
Treuerell
Tenwis
Totelles

V
Vere
Vernoun
Vescy
Verdoune
Valence
Verdeire
Vauasour
Vendore
Verlay
Valenger
Venables
Venoure
Vilan
Verland
Valers
Veirny
Vauurvile
Veniels
Verrere
Vschere
Veffay
Vanay
Vian
Verneys
Vrnall
Vnket
Vrnafull
Vasderoll
Vaberon
Valingford
Venicorde
Valiue
Viuille
Vancorde and Valenges

W
Wardebois
Ward
Wafre
Wake
Wareine
Wate
Watelin
Wateuil
Wely
Werdonell
Wespaile
Wiuell

When king William had set all things in order through the most part of the realme, he *Sim. Dunel.* deliuered the guiding thereof vnto his brother Odo, the bishop of Bayeux, and his coosine King William goeth ouer into Normandy. *Hen. Hunt. Polychron. Sim. Dun.* William Fits Osborne, whom he had made erle of Hereford. In Lent following he sailed into Normandie, leading with him the pledges, and other of the chéefest lords of the English nation: among whom, the two earles Edwine and Marchar, Stigand the archbishop, Edgar Etheling, Walteoff sonne to Siward sometime duke of Northumberland, and Agelnothus the abbat of Glastenburie were the most famous. Soone after his departing, Edricke Syluaticus. Edricke surnamed Syluaticus, sonne to Alfricke that was brother to Edricke de Streona, refusing to submit himselfe vnto the king, rebelled and rose against such as he had left in his absence to gouerne the land. Wherevpon those that laie in the castell of Hereford, as Richard Fits Scroope. Richard Fitz Scroope and others, did oftentimes inuade his lands, and wasted the goods of his farmers and tenants: but yet so often as they attempted to inuade him, they lost manie of their owne souldiers and men of war. Moreouer, the said Edricke calling to his aid the kings of the Welshmen, Bleothgent and Rithwall, about the feast of the assumption of The riuer of Wye. our Ladie, wasted the countrie of Hereford, euen to the bridge of the riuer of Wye, and obteined out of those quarters a maruellous great spoile. In the winter also following, King William returneth into England. and after king William had disposed his busines in Normandie, he returned into England, and euen then began to handle the Englishmen somewhat sharpelie, supposing thereby to kéepe them the more easilie vnder his obedience. He also took awaie from diuerse of the Nobilitie, and others of the better sort, all their liuings, and gaue the same *H. Hunt.* to his Normans. Moreouer, he raised great taxes and subsidies through the realme: nor any thing regarded th' English Nobilitie, so that they who before thought themselues to be made for euer by bringing a stranger into the realme, doo now see themselues troden vnder foot, to be despised, and to be mocked on all sides, insomuch that many of them *Matth. Paris.* were constreined (as it were for a further testimonie of seruitude and bondage) to shaue their beards, to round their heare, and to frame themselues as well in apparell as in seruice [9] and diet at their tables after the Norman manner, verie strange and farre differing from the ancient customes and old vsages of their countrie. Others vtterlie refusing to susteine such an intolerable yoke of thraldome as was dailie laid vpon them by the Normans, chose rather to leaue all both goods & lands, & after the maner of outlawes got them Englishmen withdraw them to the woods as out lawes. to the woods, with their wiues, children, and seruants, meaning from thencefoorth wholie to liue vpon the spoile of the countries adioining, and to take whatsoeuer came next to hand: wherevpon it came to passe within a while that noe man might trauell in safetie from his owne house or towne to his next neighbors, and euery quiet and honest mans house became as it were an hold and fortresse furnished for defense with bowes and arrowes, bills, polaxes, swords, clubs, and staues, and other weapons, the doores kept locked and stronglie boulted in the night season, for feare to be surprised as it had beene in time of open warr and amongst publike enimies. Praiers were said also by the maister of the house, as though they had beene in the middest of the seas in some stormie tempest, and when the windowes or doores should be shut in and closed, they vsed to saie *Benedicite*, and others to answer, *Dominus*, in like sort as the preest and his penitent were woont to doo at confession in the church.

Notwithstanding all this, K. William sought to tame & vanquish those of the English Nobilitie, who would not be at his becke. They againe on the other side made themselues strong, the better to resist him, choosing for their chéefe capteines and leaders, the earles Edwine & Edgar Etheling, who valiantlie resisted the Normans, and slue many of them with great rage and crueltie. And as they thus procéeded in their matters, king William being a politike prince, forward and painefull in his businesse, suffered them not altogither to escape cléere awaie, but did sore annoy and put them oft to remediles losses, though he abode in the meane time many laborious iournies, slaughters of his people, and damages of his person. Herevpon the English Nobilitie euer after, yea in time of peace, *Polydor.*
Anno Reg. 2.
Matth. Paris. Matth. West.
Diuers of the English Nobilitie forsake their natiue countrie. were hated of the king and his Normans, and at length were kept so short, that being mooued partlie with disdaine, and partlie with dread, they got them out of the realme, some into Scotland, some into Denmarke, others into Norway; and among these, the two earles Edwine and Marchar, with certeine bishops & others of the cleargie, besides manie also of the temporaltie, escaped into Scotland. Marleswine & Gospatricke, with a great number of other the Nobles of Northumberland, Edgar Ethling with his mother Agatha, and his sisters Christine and Margaret, chanced also to be driuen into Scotland by tempest, as they sailed towards the coasts of Germanie, pur-

posing to haue returned into Hungarie, where the said Edgar was borne: howbeit being arriued in Scotland, he found so friendlie entertainment there, that finallie Malcolme the third then king of that realme, tooke his sister Margaret to wife, and Christine became a nunne, as in the Scotish *Polydor.* chronicles more plainelie dooth appéere. King William héereby perceiuing daily how vnwilling the Englishmen were to be vnder his obeisance, was in feare of rebellious commotions; and therefore to subdue them the better, he builded foure castels, one at Notingham, Two at York, wherein he left fiue hundred men in garrison. another at Lincolne, the third at Yorke, and the fourth néere vnto Hastings, where he landed at his first comming into England.

Moreouer, to reduce the English people the sooner vnto obedience and awe, he tooke *Simon Dun.* The Conquerour taketh frō the Englishmen their armour. from them all their armour and weapons. He ordeined also that the maister of euerie houshold about eight of the clocke in the euening, should cause his fire to be raked vp ashes, his lights to be put out, and then go to bed. Besides this, to the end that euerie man might haue knowledge of the houre to go to rest, he gaue order, that in all cities, townes, and villages, where anie church was, there should a bell be roong at the said houre, which custome is still vsed euen vnto this daie, Couer few first instituted. and commonly called by the French word, *Couer few*, that is, *Rake vp the fier.*

1068. *Matth. West.* This yeare, on Whitsunday, Maud the wife of king William was crowned Queene by Aeldred archbishop of Yorke. The same yeare also was Henrie his sonn borne here in England: for his other two sonns, Robert and William, were borne in Normandie before [10] Edmond the Great. he had conquered this land. About the same time alsoe Goodwine and Edmund surnamed the great, the sonns of K. Harold, came from Ireland and landing in Somersetshire, fought with Adnothus that had beene maister of their fathers horsses whom they slue

with a great number of others, and soe haueing got this victorie, returned into Ireland, from whence they came with a great bootie which they tooke in their returne out of Cornewall, Deuonshire, and other places thereabouts. In like manner, Excester did as then rebell, and *Wil. Malm. Simon Dunelm.* likewise the countrie of Northumberland, wherevpon the king appointed one of his capteines named Robert Cumin, a right noble personage (but more valiant than circumspect) to go against the northerne people with a part of his armie, whilest he himselfe and the other part went to subdue them of Excester: where, at his comming before the citie, the citizens prepared themselues to defend their gates and wals: but after he began to make his approch to assaile them, part of the citizens repenting their foolish attempts, opened the gates, and suffered him to enter. Thus having subdued them of Excester, he gréeuouslie punished the chéefe offendors. But the countesse Gita, the sister of Sweine K. of Denmarke, and sometime wife to earle Goodwine, and mother to the last K. Harold, with diuers other that were got into that citie, found meanes to flie, and so escaped ouer into Flanders. King William hauing passed his businesse in such wise in Deuonshire, hasted backe towards Yorke, being aduertised in the waie, that the Northumbers hauing knowledge by their spials, that Robert generall of the Normans being come to Durham, did not so diligentlie cause watch and ward to be kept about the towne in the night season This chaunced the 28. of Januarie on a Wednesday. *Polydor.* as was requisite, did set vpon him about midnight, & slue the same Robert with all his companie, so that of seauen hundred which he brought with him, there was but one that escaped to bring tidings to the king their souereigne.

He heard also, how Edgar Etheling at the same time, being in the countrie, riding abroad with a troope of horsemen, and hearing of the discomfiture of those Normans, pursued them egerlie, and slue great numbers of them, as they were about to saue themselues *Polydor.*

by flight, with which newes being in no small furie, he made speed forward, and comming at the last into Northumberland, he easilie vanquished the foresaid rebels, and putting the cheefe authors of this mutinie to death, he reserued some of the rest as captiues, and of other some he caused the hands to be chopped off in token of their inconstancie and rebellious dealing. After this he came to Yorke, and there in like sort punished those that had aided Edgar, which doone, he returned to London.

1069. Sweine and Osborne hath. *Matth. Paris.* In the meane time, those Englishmen that were fled (as you haue heard) into Denmarke, by continuall sute made to Sueine then king of that realme, to procure him to make a iournie into England for recouerie of the right descended to him from his ancestors, at length obteined their purpose, in so much that king Sueine sent his sonnes Thrée hundred sailes saith *M. W.* but *Sim. Dun.* hath 240. Harold and Canutus toward England, who with a nauie of two hundred saile, in the companie of Osborne their vncle, arriued in the mouth of Humber betwéene the two later ladie daies, and there landing their people with the English outlawes, whom they had brought with them, they straightwaies marched towards Yorke, wasting and spoiling the countrie with great crueltie as they passed. Soone after also came Edgar, and such other English exiles as had before fled into Scotland, and ioined their forces with them. When the newes of these things were brought to Yorke, the people there were striken with a maruellous feare, insomuch that Aeldred the archbishop (through verie greefe and anguish of mind) departed this life. The Normans also which laie there in garrison, after they vnderstood by their spies that the enimies were come within two daies iournie of them, began not a little to mistrust the faith of the citizens, and bicause the suburbes should not be any aid vnto them, they set fire on the same, which by the hugenesse of the wind that suddenlie arose, the flame became so big, and mounted such a height, that Yorke burnt. it caught the citie also, and consumed a great part therof to ashes, togither with the minster of S. Peter, and a famous librarie belonging to the same. Herevpon the Normans and citizens in like maner were constreined to issue foorth at the same time, and [11] being vpon the enimies before they had any knowledge of their approch, were forced to trie the matter by disordered battell: whose number though it was far inferiour vnto theirs, yet they valiantlie defended themselues for a time, till being oppressed with multitudes, they were ouercome and slaine, so that there perished in this conflict, to the number Normans slaine. of three thousand of them. Manie of the Englishmen also that came with them to the field, were saued by the enimies, to the end they might gaine somewhat by their ransomes, *Simon Dun.* as William Mallet shirife of the shire, with his wife, and two of their children, Gilbert de Gaunt, and diuers other. This slaughter chanced on a saturdaie, being the nineteenth day of September; a dismall daie to the Normans.

The two brethren hauing thus obteined this victorie, went on further into the countrie of Northumberland, and brought the same wholie to their subiection, insomuch that all the north parts were at their cōmandement. Vpon this they meant to haue gone towards A sharpe winter, an enimie to warlike enterprises. London with the like attempt in the south parts, if the extreame and hard winter which chanced that yeare, had not staied their enterprise, as it did king William from assailing them; who hearing of all their dooings in the north countrie, would else full gladlie haue The Danes where they wintered. *Hen. Hunt. Polydor.* set vpon them. In the meane time, the Danes wintered in Yorkeshire, betwixt the two riuers Ouse and Trent; but so soone as the snow began to melt, and the yce to thaw and waste away, king William sped him with great hast toward his enimies into Yorkeshire, and comming to the riuer of Trent, where it falleth into Humber, he pitched his tents there, to refresh his people, for his enimies were at hand. The daie following he brought his armie into the field to fight with the Danish princes, who likewise in battell araie met them. Then began a right sore and terrible battell, continuing a long space in equall balance, till at length in one of the Danish wings the Norman horsemen had put their enimies to flight. Which when the residue of the Danes perceiued, and therewith put in a sudden feare, they likewise fled. Harold and Canutus with a band of hardie souldiers that tarried about them, retired backe (though with much a doo and great danger) vnto their ships. Edgar also, by helpe of good horses, escaped into Scotland with a few in *Matth. Paris.* his companie. Earle Walteof, who had fought most manfullie in that battell, & slaine manie Normans with his owne hands, was reconciled into the kings fauour: but the residue *Hen. Hunt. Wil. Malm.* were for the most part taken prisoners, and killed. William of Malmesburie writeth, that king William comming at that time into the north parts, besieged the citie of Yorke, and putting to flight a great armie of his enimies that came to the succour of them within, not without great losse of his owne souldiers, at length the citie was deliuered into his hands; the citizens and other that kept it, as Scots, Danes, and Englishmen, *Sim. Dunel.* being constreined thereto through lacke of vittels. Other write, how the Danes, being loden with riches and spoiles gotten in the countrie, departed to their ships before the comming of king William. Here is not to be forgotten, that (as Iohn Leland hath noted) whilest the Conquerour held siege before Yorke, at the earnest request of his wife Quéene Maud, he aduanced his nephew Alane earle of Britaine, with the gift of all those lands that sometime belonged vnto earle Edwine, the tenor of which gift insueth:

Earle Edwines lands giuen vnto Alane earle of Britaine. "Ego Gulihelmus cognomine Bastardus, do & concedo tibi nepoti meo Alano Britanniæ comiti, & hæredibus tuis in perpetuum, omnes illas villas & terras, quæ nuper fuerunt comitis Eadwini in Eborashira, cum feodis militum & alijs libertatibus & consuetudinibus, ita liberè & honorificè sicut idem Eadwinus ea tenuit. Dat. in obsidione coram ciuitate Eboraci:" that is, "I William surnamed Bastard, doo giue and grant to thee my nephue Alane earle of Britaine, and to thine heires for euer, all those townes and lands that latelie were earle Eadwines in Yorkeshire, with the knights fees and other liberties and customes, so freelie and honourablie as the said Eadwine held the same. Giuen in our seege before the citie of Yorke."

The earle of Britaine, being a man of a stout stomach, and meaning to defend that Castell of Richmont. which was thus giuen to him, built a strong castell neere to his manor of Gillingham, and named it Richmont. The first originall line of the earles of Richmont [2] that bare their [12] title of honor of this castell and towne of Richmont (as Leland hath set downe the same) is this: Eudo earle of Britaine, the sonne of Geffrey, begat three sonnes, Alane le Rous, otherwise Fregaunte, Alane the blacke, and Stephan. These three brethren after their Earle of Britaine. fathers decease, succéeded one another in the earledome of Britaine; the two elder, Alane the red and Alane the blacke died without issue. Stephan begat a sonne named Alane, who left a sonne, which was his heire named Conan, which Conan married Margaret the daughter of William king of Scotland, who bare him a daughter named Constantia, which Constantia was coupled in marriage with Geffrey sonne to king Henrie the second, who had by hir Arthur, whom his vncle King John, for fear to be depriued by him of the crowne, caused to be made awaie; as some have written. But now to returne where we *Simon Dun.*

Matth. Paris maketh mention but of Sweine and Osborne whom he calleth brethren. left touching the Danes. Simon Dunel. affirmeth, that Harold and Canute or Cnute the sonnes of Sweine king of Denmarke, with their vncle earle Osborne, and one Christianus a bishop of the Danes, and earle Turketillus were guiders of this Danish armie, & that afterwards, when king William came into Northumberland, he sent vnto earle Osborne, promising him that he would permit him to take vp vittels for his armie about the sea coastes; and further, to giue him a portion of monie, so that he should depart and returne home as soone as the winter was passed. But howsoeuer the matter went with the Danes, certain it is by the whole consent of writers, that king William hauing thus subdued his enimies in the north, he tooke so great displeasure with the inhabitants of the countrie of Yorkeshire and Northumberland, that he wasted all the land betwixt Yorke *Wil. Malms.* and Durham, so that for the space of threescore miles, there was left in maner no habitation for the people, by reason whereof it laie wast and desert for the space of nine or ten yeares. ¶ The goodlie cities with their towers and steeples set vp on a statelie height, and reaching as it were into the aire: the beautifull fields and pastures, watered with the course of sweet and pleasant riuers, if a stranger should then haue beheld, and also knowne before they were thus defaced, he would surely haue lamented: or if any old inhabitant had béene long absent, & newly returned thither, had séene this pitifull face of the countrie, he would not haue knowne it, such destruction was made through out all those quarters, whereof Yorke it selfe felt not the smallest portion. The bishop of Durham Egelwinus with his cleargie fled into holy Iland with S. Cuthberts bodie, and other iewels of the *Simon Dun.* church of Durham, where they tarried three moneths and od daies, before they returned to Durham againe. The kings armie comming into the countrie that licth betwixt the riuers Theise and Tine, found nothing but void feelds and bare walles; the people with their goods and cattell being fled and withdrawne into the woods and mountaines, if any thing were forgotten behind, these new gests were diligent inough to find it out.

Anno Reg. 4.

1070. *Polydor.* In the beginning of the spring, king William returned to London, and now after all these troubles, began to conceiue greater hatred against the Englishmen than euer before; so as doubting that hee should neuer by gentlenesse win their good willes, he now determined by a harder measure to meete with them; insomuch that he banished a great number, other some also (not a few) he spoiled of their goods, those especiallie of whom he was in hope to gaine any great portion of substance.

Thus were the Englishmen generallie in danger to lose life, lands and goods, without knowledge, or orderlie proceeding in iudgement, so that no greater miserie in the earth could be imagined, than that whereinto our nation was now fallen. He tooke from the Priuileges and fréedoms revoked. townes and cities, from the bishops sées and abbeies all their ancient priuileges and freedoms, to the end they should not onely be cut short and made weaker, but also that they (for the obteinment of their quietnesse) might redeeme the same of him for such summes of monie as pleased him to exact. Among other things, he ordeined that in time of warre *Matth. Paris.* they should aide him with armor, horsse and monie, according to that order which he should then prescribe: all which he caused to be registred, inrolled, and laid vp in his treasurie. But diuerse of the spirituall persons would not obey this ordinance, whom he banished without remorse.

[13] Stigand. Alexander bishop of Lincolne.

Polydor.

The hard deling of K. William against the Englishmen. About this time the archbishop Stigand, and Alexander bishop of Lincolne fled to Scotland, where they kept themselues close for a season. But the king still continued in his hard procéeding against the Englishmen, insomuch that now protesting how he came to the gouernance of the realme only by plaine conquest, he seized into his hands most part of euery mans possessions, causing them to redeeme the same at his hands againe, and yet reteined a propertie in the most part of them; so that those that should afterwards enioy them, should acknowledge themselues to hold them of him, in yéelding a yéerlie rent to him and his successors for euer, with certeine other prouisions, whereby in cases of forfeiture the same lands should returne to him, and his said successors againe. The like order he appointed to be vsed by other possessors of lands, in letting them forth to their The institution of the foure Termes. tenants. He ordeined also, that the Termes should be kept foure times in the yéere, in such places as he should nominate, and that the iudges shuld sit in their seuerall places to iudge and decide causes and matters in controuersie betwixt partie and partie, in manner as is vsed vnto this day. He decréed moreouer, that there should be shiriffes in euerie shire, and iustices of the peace to keepe the countries in quiet, and to sée offendors punished. Furthermore, he instituted the court of the The Excheker. Excheker, and the officers belonging to the same, as the barons, the clearks, and such other, and also the high court The Chancerie. of Chancerie.

After he had in this sort ordeined his magistrates and ministers of the lawes, he lastlie tooke order what ordinances he would haue obserued: wherevpon abrogating in maner all the ancient lawes vsed in times past, and instituted by the former kings for the good order New lawes. and quietnes of the people, he made new, nothing so equall or easie to be kept; which neuerthelesse those that came after (not without their great harme) were constreined to obserue: as though it had beene an high offense against GOD to abolish those euill lawes, which king William (a prince nothing friendly to the English nation) had first ordeined, and to bring in other more easie and tollerable. ¶ Here by the waie I giue you to note a great absurditie; namelie, that those lawes which touched all, and ought to be knowne of The lawes were written in the Norman toong. all, were notwithstanding written in the Norman toong, which the Englishmen vnderstood not; so that euen at the beginning you should haue great numbers, partlie by the iniquitie of the lawes, and partlie by ignorance in misconstruing the same, to be wrongfullie condemned: some to death, and some in the forfeitures of their goods; others were so intangled in sutes and causes, that by no means they knew how to get out, but continuallie were tossed from post to piller; in such wise that in their minds they curssed the time that euer these vnequall lawes were made.

Matters to be tried by a Iurie of 12. men. The maner for the triall of causes in controuersie, was deuised in such sort as is yet vsed. Twelue ancient men (but most commonlie vnlearned in the lawes) being of the same countie where the sute laie, were appointed by the iudges to go togither into some close chamber, where they should be shut vp, till vpon diligent examination of the matter they should agrée vpon the condemnation or acquiting of the prisoner, if it were in criminall causes; or vpon deciding in whom the right remained, if it were vpon triall of things in controuersie. Now when they were all agréed, they came in before the iudges, declaring to what agréement they were growne: which doone, the iudges opened it to the offendors or sutors, and withall gaue sentence as the qualitie of the case did inforce and require. There may happilie be (as Polydor Virgil saith) that will maintaine this maner of procéeding in the administration of iustice by the voices of a iurie, to haue béene in vse before the conquerors daies, but they are not able to prooue it by any ancient records of writers, as he thinketh: albeit by some of our histories they should séeme to be first ordeined by Ethelred or Egelred. Howbeit this is most true, that the Norman kings themselues would confesse, that the lawes deuised and made by the Conqueror were not verie equall; insomuch that William Rufus and Henrie the sonnes of the Conqueror would at all times, when they sought to purchase the peoples fauor, promise to abolish the lawes ordeined by their father, establish other more equall, and restore those which were vsed [14] in S. Edwards daies. The like kind of purchasing fauour was vsed by king Stéephen, and other kings that followed him. But now to the matter, king William hauing made these ordinances to keepe the people in order, set his mind to inrich his cofers, and therevpon caused first a tribvte to be leuied of the commons; then the abbeies to be searched, and *Matth. Paris. Matth. West.*
Wil. Mal. Wil. Thorne.
Abbeis searched. all such monie as any of the Englishmen had laid vp in the same, to be kept. Besides all this, he seized into his hands their charters of priuileges made to them by the Saxon kings of the land, and spared not so much as the iewels and plate dedicated to sacred vses. All this did he (as some write) by the counsell of the earle of Hertford.
Polydor.
Simon Dun.
Wil. Thorne.
Polydor.
Sim. Dunel.
Stigand archbishop of Canturburie depriued. Shortlie after betwixt Easter and Whitsuntide, a great synod was holden at Winchester by the bishops and cleargie, where Ermenfred the bishop of Sion or Sitten, with two cardinals Iohn and Peter sent thither from pope Alexander the second, did sit as chéefe commissioners. In this synod was Stigand the archbishop of Canturburie depriued of his bishoprike, for three speciall causes.

1 First, for that he had wrongfullie holden that bishoprike, whilest the archbishop Robert was liuing.

2 Secondlie, for that he kept the see of Winchester in his hands, after his inuestiture vnto Canturburie, which he ought not to haue doone.

3 Thirdlie, for that he had receiued the pall at the hands of pope Benedict the tenth, whom the cardinals, as one not lawfullie elected, had deposed.

Howbeit, manie writers burthen king William (who was present at this synod) for the procuring of Stigand his depriuation, to the end he might place a stranger in his roome. For as he had rooted out the English Nobilitie, and giuen awaie their land and liuings to his Normans; so meant he to turne out the English cleargie from bearing any office of honor within the realme, which meaning of his did well appeare at his councell, wherin Agelmarus bishop of Thetford was one that was deposed.

Simon Dun. Matt. Paris. diuers bishops, abbats, and priors were deposed, and Normans preferred to their places. Stigand after his depriuation was kept in perpetuall prison at Winchester, till he died, and yet (as some write) the same Stigand was an helper vnder hand for king William to atteine the crowne.

Thomas a canon of Bayeux made archbishop of Yorke.

Lanfranke consecrated archbishop of Canturburie.

Matth. Westm. hath the eight Kal. of Maie, but *Wil. Mal.* and *Eadmerus* the fourth Kal. of September.

Wil. Mal. Eadmerus. In the feast of Pentecost next insuing, the king being at Windsor, gaue the archbishoprike of Yorke vnto one Thomas, a canon of Bayeux, and to Walkelme one of his chaplins he gave the Bishoprike of Winchester. After this, calling one Lanfranke an Italian from Caen where he was abbat, he made him archbishop of Canturburie, who was consecrated there in the feast of S. John Baptist, in the yeare folowing, which was after the birth of our Sauiour 1071.

An. Reg. 5. 1071. The foresaid Thomas was the fiue and twentith bishop that had gouerned in that see of Yorke, & Lanfranke the thrée & thirtith in the see of Canturburie. But yer long, betwixt these two archbishops there rose great contention for the primasie of their churches, in so much that the archbishop of Yorke appealed to Rome, where they both appeared personallie before pope Alexander, in whose presence Lanfranks cause was so much fauoured, that not onelie the foresaid Thomas, but also Remigius the bishop of Dorchester were for reasonable causes depriued of their crosiers and rings: and Lanfranke at their humble request was a meane to the pope for them in the end, that they might be restored to their staues, which was accordinglie obteined. For when the pope heard Lanfranke declare in their fauour, how necessarie their seruice might be to the king, in the establishment of his new gotten kingdome, he said to Lanfranke; "Well, looke you then to the matter, you are the father of that countrie, and therefore consider what is expedient to be done therein: their staues which they haue surrendered, there they be, take them, and dispose them as you shall thinke most profitable for the aduancement of the christian religion in that countrie. " Wherevpon, Lanfranke tooke the staues, and deliuered them to the former possessours, and so were they in the popes presence restored to their former dignities. One cause why Thomas was depriued (as some writers saie) was, for that he had holpen duke William towards his iournie into England when he came to conquer it, for the which pleasure to him then shewed, the duke promised [15] him a bishoprike, if euer he obteined victorie ouer the English: an other cause, for that he was a priests sonne. Now, when the pope vnderstood the full ground of their *Wil. Malm.* contention to be for the primasie of the two sees, Canturburie and Yorke, and had heard what could be alledged on both sides, he remitted the determination thereof to the king and bishops of England, that by the histories and records of the land, the matter might be tried, iudged, and ordered.

Wherefore, at their comming home, and after long debating and discussing of the cause (as in William Marleburgh it appeareth more at large) at a synod holden at Windsor, in Anno Reg. 6. 1072. *Matth. West.*

The subiection of the archbishoprike of Yorke, to the archbishoprike of Canterburie. yeare 1072, sentence was giuen on Lanfranks side, so that in all things concerning religion and the faith of holie church, the archbishop of Yorke should be euer subiect to the archbishop of Canturburie, and come with all the bishops of his prouince to what place soeuer the archbishop of Canturburie should summon any councell within the realme of England. Moreouer, when anie elected bishop of Canturburie was to be consecrated, the archbishop of Yorke (for the time being) should come to Canturburie, and consecrate him there. And if the archbishop of Yorke was to be installed and consecrated, then should he come to Canturburie, or to what place it should please the archbishop of Canturburie to assigne, and there to be confirmed of him, taking an oth with profession of due *Polydor.* The archbishop of Yorke, acknowledged primate of all Scotland. obedience vnto the higher see. Now, as the said Thomas of Yorke did yéeld obedience to Lanfranke of Canturburie, so likewise the elect bishop of Glascow in Scotland named Michaell, was soone after consecrated of the foresaid Thomas archbishop of Yorke, and made an oth of obedience vnto the said archbishop, as to the primate of all Scotland: and after him Tothade the bishop of S. Andrewes did the like, by commandement of Malcolme the third of that name king of Scotland, and Margaret his wife, who thought good by this recognisance of obedience and dutie, so to prouide against further inconuenience to come, that hereafter, one of the bishops of their realme should not take vpon them to consecrate an other: or doo any thing contrarie to the ancient decrées of the old fathers, that might be preiudiciall to the authoritie of the archbishop of Yorke, at whose appointment *Ranulph Cestren.* lib. 1. cap. 57. & lib. 7. cap. 2. those and the like things were accustomed to be doone. In this controuersie (or the like) it is left written, that in a court held at Rome (the time is not mentioned) the pope perceiuing the strife betwéene these two prelats to be but for the highest place or primasie in the church; he solemnlie gaue sentence, that the sée of Yorke should haue in title Primas Angliæ, & Canturburie Primas totius Angllæ, which titles doo yet remain to them both.

But to leaue this, and to speake of other things which chanced in the meane time that this controuersie depended betwixt the two archbishops, I find that Edwin and Marchar earles of Mertia and Northumberland, hauing of late obteined pardon for their former misdemeanor, & reconciled to the king, began now so much to mislike the state of the world againe, as euer they did before. For perceiuing how the Englishmen were still oppressed with thraldome & miserie on ech hand, they conspired, & began a new rebellion, *Matt. Paris.* but with verie ill successe, as shall herafter appeare. The king vnderstanding of their dealings, and being not onelie armed throughlie with temporall force, but also endued with the spirituall power of his archbishop Lanfranke (who aided him in all that he might, for the suppressing of those rebels) wasted the countries excéedinglie, where he vnderstood that they had gotten any reléefe, minding vtterlie to vanquish them with sword, fire and hunger, or by extreame penurie to bring them vnder. They on the other part make as stout resistance; and perceiuing that it stood them vpon, either to vanquish or to fall into vtter ruine, they raise a mightie strong host, and make Edgar Etheling their capteine, a comelie gentleman and a valiant, in whome also the whole hope of the English nation was reposed, as appeareth by this his accustomed byword, Edgar Etheling Englands dearling. Amongst other noble men that were chiefe dooers in the assembling of this armie, Frederike abbat of S. Albons, a prelate of great wealth and no lesse puissance, was a principall.

[16] The king perceiuing his estate to be now in no small danger, is in a great perplexitie what to doo, in the end, he counselleth with the said Lanfranke archbishop of Canturburie, how he might remedie the matter; who told him that in such a desperate case, the best waie for him should be to séeke by faire words and friendly offers to pacifie the English Nobilitie, which by all meanes possible would neuer ceasse to molest him in the recouerie of their liberties. Wherevpon he made meanes to come to some agréement with them, and so well the matter procéeded on his side, that the Englishmen being deceiued through his faire promises, were contented to common of peace, for which purpose they came also vnder the conduct of the abbat Frederike vnto Berkamsted, where (after much reasoning and debating of the matter for the conclusion of amitie betwixt them) king William in the presence of the archbishop Lanfranke and other of his lords, tooke a personall oth vpon all the relikes of the church of S. Albons, and the holie euangelists (the abbat Frederike ministring the same vnto him) that he would from thencefoorth obserue and kéepe the good and ancient approoued lawes of the realme, which the noble kings of England his predecessors had made and ordeined heretofore; but namelie those of S. Edward, which were supposed to be most equall and indifferent.

The peace being thus concluded, and the Englishmen growne thereby to some hope of further quietnesse, they began to forsake their alies, and returned each one, either to his owne possessions, or to giue attendance vpon the king. But he warilie cloking his inward purpose, notwithstanding the vnitie latelie made, determineth particularlie to assaile his enimies (whose power without doubt so long as it was vnited, could not possiblie be ouercome, as he thought) and being now by reason of this peace disseuered and dispersed, he thought it high time to put his secret purposes in execution: wherevpon taking them at vnwares and thinking of nothing lesse than warres and sudden inuasion, he imprisoneth manie, killeth diuers, and pursueth the residue with fire and sword, taking awaie their goods, possessions, lands, and inheritances, and banishing them out of the realme. In the meane time, those of the English Nobilitie, which could escape this his outragious tyrannie, got awaie, and amongst other, Edgar Etheling fled againe into Scotland: but Edwin was slaine of his owne souldiers, as he rode toward Scotland. Earle Marchar, and *Ran. Higa. H. Hunt. Matth. Paris.* one Hereward, with the bishop of Durham named Egelwinus, got into the Ile of Elie, in purpose there to defend themselues from the iniurie of the Normans, for they tooke the place (by reason of the situation) to be of no small strength. Howbeit king William endeuouring to cut them short, raised a power, and stopped all the passages on the east side, and on the west part he made a causie through the fennes, of two miles in length, whereby *Polydor. Hen. Hunt. Matth. Paris.* he got vnto them, and constreined them to yeeld. But Marchar, or (as others haue) Hereward, foreséeing the imminent danger likelie to take effect, made shift to get owt of the Ile by bote, and so by spéedie flight escaped into Scotland. *Simon Dun.* The bishop of Durham being taken, was sent to the abbey of Abingdon, to be kept as prisoner, where he was so sparinglie fed, Some write that he was so stubborne-harted, that after he knew he should remaine in perpetuall prison, he refused his meate, and so pined himselfe to death. that within a short space he died for hunger.

In this meane time, and whilest king William was thus occupied in rooting out the English, Malcolme king of Scotland had wasted the countries of Theisedale, Cleueland, and the lands of S. Cuthbert, with sundrie other places in the north parts. Wherevpon Gospatrike being latelie reconciled to the king & made earle of Northumberland, was sent against him, who sacked and destroied that part of Cumberland which the said Malcolme by violence had brought vnder his subiection. At the same time Malcolme was at Weremouth, beholding the fire which his people had kindled in the church of Saint Peter to burne vp the same, and there hearing what Gospatrike had doone, he tooke such displeasure thereat, that he commanded his men they should leaue none of the English nation A bloudie cōmandment executed vpon the English by the Scots. aliue, but put them all to the sword without pity or compassion, so oft as they came to hand. The bloudie slaughter which was made at this time by the Scots, through that cruell commandement of Malcolme, was pitifull to consider, for women, children, old and yong, went all one way: howbeit, manie of those that were strong and able to serue for [17] drudges and slaues, were reserued, and carried into Scotland as prisoners, where they remained manie yeares after; in so much that there were few houses in that realme, but had one or mo English slaues and captiues, whom they gat at this vnhappie voiage. Miserable was the state of the English at that time, one being consumed of another so vnnaturallie, manie of them destroied by the Scots so cruellie, and the residue kept vnder by the king so tyrannicallie.

But to returne to the purpose in hand, king William hearing of all these things, was not a little mooued at the same, but chéefelie with Malcolme king of Scots, for that his countrie was the onelie place wherein all the mal-contents of his realme had their refuge. Wherfore, thinking to reuenge the losse of his subiects, and to bring that realme also vnto his subiection, he went thither with an huge armie, about the middle of August, where he first inuaded the bounds of Galloway, bicause he heard how the English were latelie fled *Polydor* thither. But after he had wearied his souldiers in vaine pursuit of them (who kept themselues in the mountaines and marres grounds) he gaue ouer the enterprise, and drew towards Lothiam, where king Malcolme laie with all his power, & sundrie English fugitiues, with whome he determined by battell either to end his trouble, or else to loose his *Matth. Paris.* life. Now as both the kings with their armies were readie to encounter, Malcolme began to doubt somewhat of the fiersenesse of the battell, bicause he saw the great puissance and readie willes of the English and Normans to fight, wherevpon he sent an harrold to *H. Hunt.* king William to treat of peace, wherewith he was content at the last (though with much adoo) and so a vnitie insued betwixt them, vpon these conditions; namelie, that king The king of Scots did homage to king William for Scotland. Malcolme should doo homage to king William for the realme of Scotland, and therevpon deliuer sufficient hostages: and that on the other side, king William should pardon all the English outlawes in Scotland which then rebelled against him. The place where this peace was concluded, was called Abirnethi. After this, king William returned into England, where he yer long tooke the earledome of Northumberland from Gospatrike, and *Simon Dun.* gave it to Waltheof the sonne of Siward; bicause of right it séemed to descend vnto him The kings iustice. from his father, but chéefelie from his mother Alfreda, who was the daughter of Aldred sometime earle of that countrie.

At the same time also the king caused a castell to be built at Durham, and returned to London, where he receiued aduertisement that his subiects in Normandie toward the parties [3] of Angiew had begun a rebellion against him. Heerevpon with all spéed he leuied an armie, whereof the most part consisted of English (whose seruice he liked rather in a forren countrie than in their owne) and sailed ouer into Normandie, where he easilie subdued his enemies by the valiancie of the English, whom from thenceforth he began somewhat to fauour and better thinke of than before. Yoong Edgár also grew in verie good credit with him, for though he had twise broken his oth of allegiance, and run to the Scots as a rebell, yet now of his owne motion, returning to the king and crauing pardon, he was not onelie receiued, but also highlie honoured and preferred in his court.

The yeare 1074. thrée moonks of the prouince of Mercia, purposing to restore religion after their maner within the prouince of Northumberland, came into Yorke, and required Mountcaster now Newcastell. of Hugh Fitz Baldricke (then shirife of the shire) to haue safe conduct vnto Monkaster, which afterwards hight Newcastell, and so is called to this day. These moonks, whose names were Aldwin, Alswin, and Remfred, comming vnto the foresaid place, found no token or remanent of any religious persons, which sometime had habitation there (for all was defaced and gone:) wherevpon, after they had remained there a while, they remooued to Jarrowe, where finding the ruines of old decaied buildings and churches, perteining in times past to the moonks that there inhabited, they had such assistance at the hands of Walkher bishop of Durham, that at length, by the diligent trauell and sute of these moonks, three monasteries were newlie founded and erected in the north parts, one at Durham, an other at Yorke, and the third at Whitby. For you must consider, that [18] by the inuasion of the Danes, the churches and monasteries throughout Northumberland were so wasted and ruinated, that a man could scarselie find a church standing in all that countrie, as for those that remained, they were couered with broome or thatch: but as for any abbey or monasterie, not one was left in all the countrie, neither did any man (for the space of two hundred yeares) take care for the repairing or building vp of any thing in decaie, so that the people of that countrie wist not what a moonke ment, and if they saw any, they woondered at the strangenesse of the sight.

An. Reg. 9.

1075. Rafe Earle of Cambridge.
Matth. West. Matth. Paris. Hen. Hunt. Simon Dun.
A rebellion raised against K. William. Whilest the king remained thus in Normandie, Roger earle of Hereford (contrarie to the kings mind and pleasure) married his sister vnto Rafe earle of Cambridge, or (as other haue) Northfolke, and withall began a new conspiracie against him. Amongst other also of the associats, earle Walteof the sonne of earle Siward was one, who afterward mistrusting the successe of this deuise, first vttered it to archbishop Lanfranke, and by his aduice sailed ouer into Normandie, and there disclosed the whole matter to king William: but in the meane time, the other two earles; namelie, Hereford and Cambridge had so farre procéeded in the matter, that they were vp in armour. Howbeit, Wolstan bishop of Worcester, and Egelwine abbat of Euesham, with the shirife of Worcester & Walter Lacie, so resisted the earle of Hereford, that he could not passe the Seuerne to ioine *Iohn Pike.* with the earle of Cambridge. On the other side, Odo the bishop of Bayeux, and Geffrey the bishop of Constances pursued the earle of Cambridge so narrowlie with an other armie, which they had gathered of the English and Normans, that they constreined him to flée into Britaine, whereby the rebellion was verie much appeased.

An. Reg. 10.

1076. In the meane time, the king vnderstanding by earle Walteof how the matter went in England, came ouer with all speed out of Normandie, & within a short space brought the residue of the conspirators into such a feare, that they were scattered and put to flight, without attempting anie further exploit or conspiracie against him. Manie of them also were apprehended and put to death, among whom Roger and Walteof were most famous. *H. Hunt.* Earle Walteof beheaded. And though Walteof (as yée haue heard before) disclosed the treason, yet to the end he should offend no more hereafter, he was beheaded at Winchester by the kings commandement, and his bodie hauing béene first buried in the same place where he suffered, was afterward conueied vnto Crowland, and there more honorablie interred.

This earle Walteof or Waldeue was sonne (as ye haue heard) to Siward the noble earle of Northumberland, of whose valure in the time of K. Edward the confessor ye haue heard. His son the foresaid Walteof in strength of bodie and hardinesse did, not degenerate from his father, for he was tall of personage, in sinews and musculs verie strong and mightie. In the slaughter of the Normans at Yorke, he shewed proofe of his prowesse, in striking off the heads of manie of them with his owne hands, as they came foorth of the gates singlie one by one: yet afterwards, when the king had pardoned him of all former offenses, and receiued him into fauour hée gaue to him in mariage his néece Judith the daughter of Lambert earle of Lens, sister to Stephen erle of Albermare, and with hir he Earledome of Huntingdon. had of the kings gift, all the lands and liberties belonging to the honor of Huntingdon; in consideration whereof, he assigned to hir in name of hir dower, all the lands that he held from Trent southward. Shée bare by him two daughters, Maud and Alice: We find, that he was not onlie earle of Northumberland, but also of Northampton and *Matth. Paris.* Huntingdon.

The countesse of Cambridge or Northfolke (as other haue) wife of earle Rafe, being, fled into the citie of Norwich, was besieged in the same by the kings power, which pressed the citie so sore, as it was forced for verie famine to yéeld; but yet by composition; namelie, that such as were besieged within, should depart the realme, as persons abiured and banished the land for euer. This was the end of the foresaid conspiracie. At this *Polydor. Hen. Hunt. Simon Dun. Matth. Paris.* verie time the Danes being confederate with these rebels, and by them solicited, set forth towards England vnder the leading of Cnuto, sonne to Sueno, and earle Haco, and (vnlooked for) arriue here in England with two hundred sailes. But hearing that the ciuill tumult was ended, and seeing no man readie either to countenance or encourage them in their enterprise, they sailed first into Flanders, which they spoiled, and after into their owne countrie, with little desire or will to come againe into England. King William also vnderstanding that they were thus departed, passed ouer into Britaine, and there besieged the castell of Doll that belonged to Rafe earle of Cambridge or Northfolke: but by the comming of Philip the French king, king William being vnprouided of sufficient vittels for his armie, was constreined to raise his siege, although with great losse both of men and horsses.

An. Reg. 11.

1077. *Matth. Paris.* An earthquake, a long frost, a comet. On the 27. daie of March was a generall earthquake in England, and in the winter following a frost that continued from the first of Nouember vntill the middle of Aprill. A blasing starre appeared on palme sundaie, beeing the sixteenth daie of Aprill, about six of the clocke, when the aire was faire and cleere.

Married préests. About the same season, pope Gregorie perceiuing that married préests did choose rather to run into the danger of his cursse, than to forsake their wiues, meaning to bridle them by an other prouiso, gaue commandment by his bull published abroad, that none should heare the masse of a married préest.

An. Reg. 12.

1078. *Polydor.* A synod holden at London. Bishops sées remoued. King William after his comming from the siege of Doll, remained a certeine time in quiet, during which season, Lanfranke the archbishop called a synod or counsell of the cleargie at London, wherein amongst other things it was ordeined, that certeine bishops sées should be remoued from small townes to cities of more fame, whereby it came to passe that Chichester, Exceter, Bath, Salisburie, Lincolne & Chester were honored with sees and palaces of bishops, whereas before they kept their residence at Sellewey, Kirton, Welles, Shireborne, Dorchester, and Lichfield.

Woolstan. At this synod also Woolstan bishop of Worcester was present, whom Lanfranke would haue deposed for his insufficiencie of learning; as he colourablie pretended, but indeed to pleasure the king, who faine would have placed a Norman in his roome: but (as they saie) by a miracle which he presentlie wrought, in causing his crosier staffe to sticke fast in the toome of saint Edward (to whom he protested and said he would resigne it, for that he obteined the same by his gift) he did put the king and the archbishop into such feare, that they suffered him still to enioy his bishoprike without any further vexation. These things with other (touching a reformation in the church and cleargie) being handled in this councell, it was soone after dissolued.

An. Reg. 13.

1079. *Matth. Paris. Matth. West.* In the yeare following, king William led a mightie armie into Wales, and subdued it; receiuing of the rulers and princes there their homages and hostages. About the same time, Robert the kings eldest sonne, a right worthie personage, but yet as one of nature somewhat vnstable, entered into Normandie as a rebell to his father, and by force tooke diuers places into his hands. Which he did by the practise of Philip the French king, who now began to doubt of the great puissance of king William, as foreseeing how much it might preiudice him, and the whole realme of France in time to come. Wherefore to stop the The French king setteth the sonne against the father. course of his prosperous successe, he deuised a meane to set the sonne against the father. True it is that king William had promised long afore to resigne the gouernment of Normandie vnto the said Robert his sonne. Wherevpon the yoong man, being of an ambitious nature, and now pricked forward by the sinister counsell of his adherents, seeketh to obteine that by violence, which he thought would be verie long yer he should atteine by curtesie. King William hereof aduertised, was not a little mooued against his disobedient *Simon Dun. Matth. Paris.* sonne, and curssed both him and the time that euer he begat him. Finallie, raising an armie, he marched towards him, so that they met in the field. Assoone as the one came in sight of the other, they encountred at a place called Archenbraie, and whilest the battell was at the hottest, and the footmen most busied in fight, Robert appointed a power of horssemen to breake in upon the réereward of his enemies; & he himselfe following after with all his might, chanced among other to haue a conflict with his owne father, so that thrusting him through the arme with his lance, he bare him beside his horsse, and [20] The sonne ouerthroweth the father. ouerthrew him to the ground. The king being falne, called to his men to remount him. Robert perceiuing by his voice that it was his father, whom he had vnhorssed, spéedilie alighted, and tooke him vp, asking him forgiuenesse for that fact, and setting him vp on his owne horsse, brought him out of the prease, and suffered him to depart in safetie. King William being thus escaped out of that present danger, and séeing himselfe not able *Simon Dun.* to resist the puissance of his enimies, left the field to his son, hauing lost many of his men which were slaine in battell and chace, besides a great number that were hurt and *Matth. Paris.* wounded, among whom his second sonne William surnamed Rufus or Red, was one; and therefore (as some write) he bitterlie curssed his son Robert, by whom he had susteined such iniurie, losse, and dishonor. Howbeit, other write, that for the courtesie which his sonne shewed, in releeuing and helping him out of danger, when he was cast off The father and the sonne made friends. his horsse, he was mooued with such a fatherlie affection, that presentlie after they were made friends, the father pardoned his sonne all his former offenses, and therevpon found him euer after more tractable and obedient than before.

An. Reg. 14.
1080. *Simon Dunel.* After this battell, king William being thus accorded with his sonne, returned with him into England, and immediatlie sent him against Malcolme king of Scotland, who hauing broken the truce in time of the trouble betwixt king William and his sonne, had doone much hurt by forraies vpon the English borders, wasting all Northumberland euen to the riuer of Tine. Howbeit, when he heard that Robert approched with his armie towards him, he retired into Scotland. Robert Curthuze then lodged with his armie vpon the The foundation of New castell vpon Tine, which before that season was called Moncaster. banks of the riuer of Tine, where he began the foundation of a castell, whereof the towne Newcastell did after take both beginning and name, for before this season it was called Moncaster.

About the same time, Odo the bishop of Bayeux was sent to Northumberland, to reuenge the death of Walkher bishop of Durham, whom not long before the people of Northumberland had slaine in a tumult. The occasion of his death grew by the death of *Simon Dun.* one Liulfus, a noble man of those quarters, and déerelie beloued of the people, bicause he was descended of honorable parentage, and had married the ladie Algitha daughter vnto earle Alered, and sister to Alfleda the mother of earle Walteof.

This Liulfus, a man of great possessions through England, now that the Normans ruled in all places, quietlie withdrew himselfe vnto Durham, and grew into such familiaritie and credit with the bishop, that touching the order of temporall matters, he would doo nothing without his aduice. Whereat Leofwin the bishops chapline conceiued such enuie (for that he was not so often called to counsell as before) that in the end he procured by his malicious meanes one Gilbert (to whom the bishop had committed the rule of the earledome) to murther the said Liulfus by night in his manor place not farre from Durham. Whereof the bishop hauing vnderstanding, and knowing that the matter would be gréeuouslie taken of the people, sent out letters and messengers into the countrie, offering to purge himselfe of the slaughter of this man, according to the order of the canon lawes: howbeit he did nothing lesse. Among other things concerning his purgation, he said that he had banished Gilbert and others, (who had committed the murther) out of Northumberland. Hervpon the malice of the people was kindled against him. For when it was knowne that he had receiued the murtherers into his house, and fauoured them as before, they stomached the matter highlie: insomuch that when by the trauell of those that went to and fro betwixt the bishop and the kinsfolks of Liulfus, a daie was appointed, on the which the bishop should come to farther communication with them at Gateshead, he repaired thither according to his promise, but refusing to talke with them abroad, he kept himselfe still within the church, and sent foorth such of his counsell as should commune with them. But when the people that were there gathered in great numbers, had signified in plaine words that he should either come foorth and shew himselfe amongst them, or else that they should fire the place where he sat: he caused Gilbert to go foorth vnto them first, whom they slue, and his partakers also that issued [21] out of the church with him for his defense. But when the peoples furie was not so quenched, the bishop himselfe casting the skirts of his gowne ouer his face, came likewise foorth, and was immediatlie slaine of the people. After this, they set the church on fire, bicause Leofwine the bishops chapline and others were yet within, and refused to come foorth: howbeit in the end, being compelled by the rage of the fire to come out, the said Leofwine was also slaine and hackt in péeces (as he had well deserued) being the ringleader of all the mischéefe.

Note the sequele of the neglect of iustice in the former storie. ¶ Thus maie we sée what followed of the neglecting of iustice in the bishop: for if he either banished Gilbert and other his complices (accordinglie as he pretended to doo) or otherwise had séene due punishment executed against them, the peoples rage had neuer proceeded so far as it did: for they could not persuade themselues, but that the bishop was guiltie and priuie to Liulfus death, sith he had receiued the murtherers into his house, the verie same night in which the fact was done, and kept them still about him, which his bearing with them cost him his owne life. But now to the historie.

When bishop Odo was come into those parties to reuenge the bishops death with an armie (as we haue said) he sore afflicted the countrie, by spoiling it on euerie side with great crueltie. Here king William placed and displaced diuerse rulers ouer the Northumbers: *Sim. Dunel.*

Copsi. for first he appointed one Copsi to haue the rule of that countrie, in place of Marchar who before had held the same. This Copsi expelled Osulfe the sonne of earle Edulfe brother to earle Aldred, which Osulfe was substitute vnto the earles Edwine and Marchar, who although he was driuen out of his gouernement by Copsi, yet recouering his forces againe, he slue the same Copsi as he entred into the church of Newburne. But within a few moneths after, the same Osulfe (as he ran with his horsse against a theefe) was thrust through the bodie with a speare, which the theefe held in Gospatrike. his hand, and so died. Then Gospatrike was assigned by king William to haue the gouernement there: whose mother Aldgitha was daughter to Vthred sometime earle of Northumberland begotten vpon Elfgiua the daughter of king Egelred.

Some write, that Gospatrike purchased the earledome of king William, and so held it, till the king tooke it from him againe, and then gaue it vnto earle Walteof or Waldeue. Next after him Walkher the foresaid bishop of Durham had the whole administration committed to him, but (after he was slaine as yée haue heard) one Alberike Robert Mulbray earle of Northumberland. ruled that countrie, and lastlie, Robert Mulbray a right noble personage (for his wisedome and valiancie highlie renowmed with all men) was created earle of Northumberland, and gouerned the people of those parties in such politike and wise order, that during his time, it is hard to saie, whether his quietnesse or the obedience of the people was greater.

The foundation of vniuersitie colledge in Oxford. An. Reg. 15.
1081. In like manner, after the foresaid Walkher; one William was created bishop of Durham, who was the originall founder of vniuersitie colledge in Oxford, and by whose assistance, the moonkes gaping both for riches, ease, and possessions, found the means to displace the secular priests of the colledge of Durham, that they might get into their roomes, as they did indeed soone after, to their great gaine and aduantage. But to returne againe to the course of the historie. Shortlie after the reuenge of the death of An. Reg. 16.
1082 Odo suspected and banished. Walkher bishop of Durham, the fornamed bishop Odo, the kings brother was suspected of some vntruth and sinister dealing, wherevpon he was sent as a banished man into Normandie, or rather (as other write) committed to prison, where he remained, not as a clerke, but as a baron of the realme; for he was both bishop and earle of Kent.

An. Reg. 17.
1083. The king hauing at length obtained some rest from wars, practised by sundrie meanes to inrich his cofers, and therefore raised a tribute through out the whole kingdome; for the better leuieng whereof, he appointed all the subiects of his realme to be numbred, all the cities, townes, villages, and hamlets to be registred, all the abbies, monasteries, [22] and priories to be recorded. Moreouer, he caused a certificat to be taken of euerie mans substance, and what he might dispend by the yeare; he also caused their names to be written which held knights fees, and were bound thereby to serue him in Plow land. the wars. Likewise he tooke a note of euerie yoke of oxen, & what number of plow lands, and how manie bondmen were within the realme. This certificat being made & brought vnto him, gaue him full vnderstanding what wealth remained among the English people. Herevpon he raised his tribute, taking six shillings for euerie hide of land through out this realme, which amounted to a great masse of monie when it was all brought togither into his Excheker. *Geruasius Tilberiensis.*

The true definition of a hide of land. ¶ Here note by the waie, that an hide of land conteineth an hundred acres, and an acre conteineth fortie perches in length, and foure in bredth, the length of a perch is sixtéene foot and an halfe: so that the common acre should make 240. perches; & eight hides or 800. acres is a knights fée, after the best approued writers and plaine demonstration. Those therefore are deceiued, that take an hide of land to conteine twentie acres (as William Lambert hath well noted in his De priscis Anglorum legibus) where he expoundeth the meaning of the old Saxon termes perteining to the lawes.

But to procéed & come, a little after the temporals dealing, to some of the spirituall affaires. It hapned about the same time, that when king William had finished the rating An. Reg. 18.
1084. *Wil. Malm. Simon Dun.*
Thurston abbat of Glastenburie.
William of Fescampe. of his subiects, that there rose a strife betwixt Thurstane abbat of Glastenburie a Norman, and the moonkes of that house. One cause thereof was, for that the abbat would haue compelled them to haue left the plaine song or note for the seruice which pope Gregorie had set foorth, and to haue vsed an other kind of tune deuised by one William of Fescampe: beside this, the said abbat spent and wasted the goods that belonged to the house, in riot, leacherie, and by such other insolent meanes (withdrawing also from the moonkes their old accustomed allowance of diet) for the which

they first fell *Hen. Hunt. Wil. Malm.* have two slaine and xiiij hurt. at altercation in words, and afterwards to fighting. The abbat got armed men about him, and falling vpon the moonkes, slue thrée of them at the high altar, and wounded xviij. Howbeit the moonkes for their parts plaied the pretie men with formes and candelstickes, defending themselues *Matt. Westm.* as well as they might, so that they hurt diuers of the abbats adherents, and droue them out of the quier.

In the end, complaint hereof was brought to the king, by whose iudgement the matter was so ordered, that Thurstane lost his roome, and returned vnto Caen in Normandie from whence he came, and the moonkes were spred abroad into diuerse houses of religion through the realme, Glastenburie being replenished with more quiet persons, and such as were supposed readier to praie than to quarell, as the other did: yet is it said, that in the time of William Rufus this Thurstane obteined the rule of that abbeie againe for fiue hundred pounds.

Sim. Dunel. Hen. Marle. Matth. Paris. There be which write, that the numbring of men and of places, the valuation of goods and substance, as well in cattell as readie monie, was not taken till about the xix. yéere of this kings reigne (although the subsidie afore mentioned was gathered about two yeares before of euerie hide of land as yée haue heard) and that the certificat hereof *Hen. Marle. Simon Dun.* An. Reg. 19. being inrolled, was put into the kings treasurie at Winchester, in the xix. yeare of his reigne, and not in the xvj. But in what yeare soeuer it was, and howsoeuer the writers agrée or disagree herein; certaine it is, that the same was exacted, to the great gréefe and impouerishment of the people, who sore lamented the miserable estate whereinto they *Polydor. Matth. Paris.* were brought, and hated the Normans in their harts to the verie death. Howbeit, the more they grudged at such tolles, tallages, customes, and other impositions wherewith they were pressed; the more they were charged and ouerpressed. The Normans on the other side The Conquerour séeketh to kéepe the English men low. with their king perceiuing the hatred which the English bare them, were sore offended, and therefore sought by all meanes to kéepe them vnder. Such as were called to be iustices, were enimies to all iustice; wherevpon greater burdens were laid vpon the English, *Polydor.* [23] insomuch that after they had béene robbed and spoiled of their goods, they were also debarred of their accustomed games and pastimes. For where naturallie (as they doo vnto this daie) they tooke great pleasure in hunting of déere, both red and fallow, in the The forrests seized into the kings hands. *Matth. Paris.* woods and forrests about without restraint, king William seizing the most part of the same forests into his owne hands, appointed a punishment to be executed vpon all such offendors; namelie, to haue their eies put out. And to bring the greater number of men in danger of those his penall lawes (a pestilent policie of a spitefull mind, and sauoring altogither of his French slauerie) he deuised meanes how to bréed, nourish, and increase the multitude of déere, and also to make roome for them in that part of the realme which lieth betwixt Salisburie and the sea southward: he pulled downe townes, villages, churches, and other buildings for the space of 30. miles, to make thereof a forrest, which at this New forrest. daie is called New forrest. The people as then sore bewailed their distres, & greatlie lamented that they must thus leaue house & home to the vse of sauage beasts. Which *Matth. Paris.* An earthquake.

Polydor. crueltie, not onelie mortall men liuing here on earth, but also the earth it selfe might seeme to detest, as by a woonderfull signification it séemed to declare, by the shaking and roaring of the same, which chanced about the 14. yeare of his reigne (as writers haue recorded.) There be that suppose how the king made that part of the realme waste and barren vpon a policie, to the intent that if his chance were to be expelled by ciuill wars, and he compelled to leaue the land, there should be no inhabitants in that part of the Ile to resist his arriuall vpon his new returne.

1085. *Simon Dun.*
A rumor spred of the coming of the Danes. But to go foorth with our purpose. About the same time, a rumor was spred in England that Sueine king of Denmarke meant to inuade England with a puissant armie, hauing the assistance of the earle of Flanders whose daughter he had maried. Whervpon king William being then in Normandie, reteined a great power of French soldiers, both archers and footmen which togither with his Normans he brought ouer into England in haruest season, and meaning to disburthen himselfe of the charge of their keeping, he caused their finding and wages to be borne by the lords and peeres of the realme, by the shirifs of shires, and other officers. Howbeit, when he vnderstood that the Danes changed Anno 20. their purpose, and would not hold on their iourneie, he dismissed part of his power, and sent them home againe, keeping the residue all the winter with him in England, readie for his defense, if anie rebellion or other necessitie should befall.

1086. The same yeare, he kept his Christmasse at Glocester, and made his sonne Henrie knight at Westminster in Whitsunwéeke insuing. Shortlie after, calling togither aswell *Matth. West.*
An oth taken to be true to the king. 1087. lords spirituall as temporall he caused them, all to sweare fealtie to him and his heires after him in the possession of this kingdome.

Great sickenes reigning. Murren of cattell.

Matth. West.
Paules church burned.
Simon Dun. Ran. Higd. Simon Dun. About this season, the people in all places were pitifullie plaged with burning feuers, which brought manie to their end: a murren also came to their cattell, whereof a woonderfull number died. At the same time (which is more maruellous) tame foules, as hens, géese, & peacocks, forsaking their owners houses, fled to the woods and became wild. Great hurt was doone in manie places of the realme by fire, and speciallie in

London, where vpon the 7. daie of Julie a sudden flame began, which burnt Paules church, and a great part or the citie downe to the verie ground.

Now when K. William had taken the oth of fealtie and loialtie of all his lords, Edgar Etheling, who was reconciled vnto his fauour (as you haue heard) obteining licence of him to depart the realme for a season, sailed into Puglia with two hundred souldiers: of whose acts there and returne into England I spare to speake, bicause I find little or nothing of moment recorded. And now king William, who hauing brought the Englishmen An. Reg. 21. so lowe and bare, that little more was to be got out of their hands, went once againe ouer into Normandie with an huge masse of monie, where soone after he fell sicke, so that he was constrained to keepe his bed longer than he had beene accustomed to doo, whereat Philip the French king in iesting manner said, that king William his cousine laie *Wil. Malm. Matth. Paris.* now in childbed (alluding belike to his big bellie, for he was verie corpulent) and withall [24] added; "Oh what a number of candels must I prouide to offer vp at his going to church! certeinelie I thinke that 100000. will not suffice," &c. This frumping spéech so moued the *Wil. Malm. Ran. Higd.* king, that he made this answere: "Well, I trust when I shall be churched, that our cousine shall be at no such cost, but I will helpe to find him a thousand candels myselfe, and light them too, to some of their paines, if God grant me life." Which promise he bound with an oth, and in déed performed. For in Julie next insuing, when their corne, fruit, and He inuadeth France.

Gemeticensis.
The citie of Maunt burnt by K. William.
Matth. West. Matth. Paris. grapes were most florishing, and readie for the sickle, he entered France with a great armie, set fire on manie of their cities and townes in the west side of that countrie, and came at last to the citie of Maunt, which he burnt with the church of our ladie, and an ankresse inclosed in the wall thereof as an holie closet, for the force of the fire was such as all went to wrecke. In this heat king William tooke such a sicknesse (which was likewise aggrauated by the fall of an horsse as he rode to and fro, bicause he was not able to trauell on foot about his palace by reason of his disease) that cost him his life; so King William departed this life.

Simon Dun. Matth. West.
The lix. of his age hath *Wil. Malm.* that when he had ordeined his last will, and taken order for the staie of things after his decease, he departed this life on the 9. day of September, in the yeare after the birth of our Saviour 1087. and 74. (as Polydor saith) of his age, hauing gouerned Normandie about 51. yeres, and reigned ouer England 20. yeares, ten monethes, and 28. daies (as all writers doo report.)

He set all prisoners at libertie saith *Wil. Malm.*

Polydor. Not long before his death, he released his brother Odo bishop of Bayeux out of prison, Marchar earle of Northumberland, and Wilnotus the sonne of king Harold, or (as some say) his brother. Moreouer he repented him (as some say) when he lay on his death bed, of his cruell dealing with the English, considering that by them he had atteined to such honour and dignitie, as to weare the crown and scepter of a kingdome: but whether he did so or not, or that some moonke deuised the excuse in fauour of the prince: surely he was a puissant prince, and though his time was troublesome, yet he was right fortunate in all his attempts. Againe, if a man shall consider that in a strange realme he could make such a conquest, and so exactlie and readilie assure the same to his heires, with new lawes, orders and constitutions (which are like for euer to endure) he would thinke it a thing altogither void of credit. Yet so it was, and so honourable were his dooings in the sight of the world, that those kings, which succeeded sithens his death, begin their account at him, as from one that had by his prudence renewed the state of the realme, and instituted an other forme of regiment, in atchiuing whereof he did not so much pretend a rightfull challenge by the grant of his coosine king Edward the Confessor, as by the law of armes and plaine conquest, than the which (as he supposed) there could be no better title.

Herevpon also those that haue sithens succeeded him, vse the same armes as peculiar to the crowne of England, which he vsed in his time; namelie, three lions passant He bare but two lions or rather leopards as some thinke. gold in a field gewels (as Polydor writeth) the three floure delices were since that time annexed thereto by Edward the third, by reason of his claime to the crowne of France, whereof hereafter ye shall heare. Among other greeuances which the English susteined by the hard deling of the Conquerour, this is to be remembered, that he brought Jewes into this land from Rouen, and appointed them a place to inhabit and occupie.

Polydor. There be that write, how the inconstancie of the English people by their oft rebellions occasioned the king to be so rough and rigorous against them; wheras (of his naturall disposition and proper inclination) he was rather gentle and courteous than sharpe and cruell. But sith he continued his extremitie euen to his last daies, we may rather beléeue, that although from his childhood he shewed some tokens of clemencie, bountie, and liberalitie; yet by following the wars, and practising to reigne with sternenesse, he became so inured therewith, that those peaceable vertues were quite altered in him, and in maner clearelie quenched. He was indued with a certeine stoutnesse of courage and skill in feats of warre, which good hap euer followed: he was frée from lecherous lusts, without suspicion of bodilie vices, quicke of wit, desirous of honor, painefull, [25] watchfull, and able to tolerate heat and cold, though he were tall of stature, and verie grosse of bodie.

Toward the end of his daies he waxed verie deuout, and became desirous to aduance the state of the church, insomuch that he builded thrée abbeies in three seuerall places, endowing them with faire lands and large possessions, one at the place where he vanquished king Harold, fiue miles from Hastings, which he named Battell, of the field there fought: the other at Celby in Yorkeshire: and the third in Normandie at Caen, where his wife Quéene Maud had builded a nunnerie, which Maud died in the yéere 1084, before the decease of the king hir husband.

After his death, his bodie was buried in Caen, in S. Stephans church; but before it They gaue him an hundred pound, saith *Hen. Marle.* could be committed to the ground, the executors were constreined to agree with the lord of the soile where the church stood, which (as he said) the king in his life time had iniuriouslie taken from him, and gaue him a great summe of monie to release his title.

¶ By this we may consider the great miserie of mans estate, in that so mightie a prince could not haue so much ground after his death as to couer his dead corps, without dooing iniurie to another. This also may be a speciall lesson for all men, and namelie for princes, noblemen, and gentlemen, who oftentimes to enlarge their owne commodities, doo not regard what wrong they offer to the inferiour sort.

The said king William had by Maud his wife the daughter of Baldwine earle of Flanders, foure sonnes, Robert surnamed Curthose (vnto whome he bequeathed the duchie of Normandie) Richard who died in his youth, William surnamed Rufus, to whom he gaue by testament the realme of England, and Henrie surnamed Beauclerke for his cunning, knowledge and learning, vnto whom he bequethed all his treasure and mooueable goods, with the possessions that belonged to his mother. Besides these foure sonnes, he *Hen. Marle.* had also by his said wife fiue daughters, Cecilie, who became a nunne; Constance, who was married to Alane duke of Britaine; Adela, who was giuen in mariage to Stephan earle of Blois (of whom that Stephan was borne which reigned after Henrie the first) Adeliza, who was promised in mariage to Harold king of England (as before you haue heard) but she died yer she was maried either to him, or to any other, and so likewise did the fift, whose name I can-

not reherse.

Iohn Rous. But to conclude, though king William held the English so vnder foot, that in his daies almost no Englishman bare any office of honor or rule in his time, yet he somewhat fauoured the citie of London, and at the earnest sute of William a Norman then bishop of that see, he granted vnto the citizens the first charter, which is written in the Saxon toong, sealed with greene wax, and expressed in viij. or ix. lines at the most, exemplified according to the copie, and so printed, as followeth.

"Williem King grets Williem Bisceop & Godfred Porterefan, & ealle ya Burghwarn binnen London Frencisce, & Englise frendlice, & Ickiden eoy, yeet ic wille yeet git ben ealra weera lagayweord, ye get weeran on Eadwerds daege kings. And ic will yeet aelc child by his fader yrfnume, aefter his faders daege. And ic nelle ge wolian, yeet aenig man eoy aenis wrang beode. God eoy heald."

"Wilhelmus rex salutat Wilhelmum Episcopum, & Goffridum Portegrefium, & omnem Burghware infra London Frans. & Angl. amicabiliter. Et vobis notum facio, quòd ego vole quòd vos sitis omni lege illa digni qua fuistis Edwardi diebus regis. Et volo quòd omnis puer sit patris sui hæres post diem patris sui. Et ego nolo pati quòd aliquis homo aliquam iniuriam vobis inferat. Deus vos saluet."

Matth. Paris. Hen. Hunt. But howsoeuer he vsed the rest of the English, this is recorded of some writers, that by his rigorous proceedings against them, he brought to passe that the countrie was so rid of theeues and robbers, as that at length a maid might haue passed through the land with a bag full of gold, and not haue met with any misdooer to haue bereft hir of the same: a thing right strange to consider, sith in the beginning of his reigne there were such routs [26] of outlawes and robbers, that the peaceabler people could not be safelie possessed of their owne houses, were the same neuer so well fortified and defended.

Iohn Rous. Hen. Marle. Among manie lawes made by the said William,

this one is to be remembred, that such as forced any woman, should lose their genitals.

Salisburie vse. In this kings daies also liued Osmond the second bishop of Salisburie, who compiled the church seruice, which in times past they commonlie called after Salisburie vse.

Shooting. The vse of the long bowe (as Iohn Rous testifieth) came first into England with this king William the Conquerour: for the English (before that time) vsed to fight with axes and such hand weapons: and therefore in the oration made by the Conquerour before he gaue battel to king Harold, the better to encourage his men, he told them they should encounter with enimies that wanted shot.

In the yeare of our Lord 1542. Monsieur de Castres bishop of Baieulx and abbat of Saint Estienne in Caen, caused the Sepulchre of this William to be opened, wherein his bodie was found whole, faire and perfect; of lims, large and big; of stature and personage, longer than the ordinarie sort of men: with a copper plate fairlie gilt, and this epitaph therevpon ingrauen:

"Qui rexit rigidos Normannos, atque Britannos
Audacter vicit, fortiter obtinuit,
Et Cœnomenses virtute contudit enses,
Imperijq. sui legibus [4] applicuit,
Rex magnus parua iacet hæc Guilhelmus in urna:
Sufficit & magno parua domus domino,
Ter septem gradibus se voluerat atq. duobus
Virginis in gremio Phœbus, & hic obijt:"

that is;

"Who ouer Normans rough did rule, and ouer Britons bold
Did conquest stoutlie win, and conquest woone did stronglie hold:
Who by his valure great the fatal vprores calmed, in maine,
And to obeie his powers and lawes, the Manceaux did constraine:
This mightie king within this little vault entoomed lies,
So great a lord sometime, so small a roome dooth now suffice.

W. Patten collecteth this to be the 23. af-

ter the sun was in *Virgo*: which is the 6. of Septēber. When three times seuen and two by iust degrees the sunne had tooke
His woonted course in Virgos lap, then he the world forsooke."
Thus far William Conquerour.

Transcriber's notes

There are no footnotes in the original. The original spelling and punctuation have been retained, with the exception of obvious errors which have been corrected by reference to the 1587 edition of which the original is a transcription.

[1] Original reads 'l d'; corrected to 'led'.

[2] Original reads '(that bare their title'; opening parenthesis removed.

[3] Original reads 'the the parties'; corrected to 'the parties'.

[4] Original reads 'suilegibus'; corrected to 'sui legibus'.